# FROM RAGE TO HOPE:

# Strategies for Reclaiming Black & Hispanic Students

by

## Crystal Kuykendall

National Educational Service

Bloomington, Indiana 1992

Cover design by Joe La Mantia

Printed in the United States of America

ISBN 1-879639-22-X

# FROM RAGE TO HOPE:

## Strategies for Reclaiming Black & Hispanic Students

by

### Crystal Kuykendall

# ABOUT THE AUTHOR . . .

Crystal Kuykendall holds a Doctorate of Education and a law degree. A former primary, junior high, and senior high school teacher, Upward Bound instructor, university instructor and guidance counselor, she is a member of the Bar of the District of Columbia and is president and general counsel of her own firm, Kreative and Innovative Resources for Kids, Inc. (K.I.R.K. Inc.). She also has served as executive director of the National Alliance of Black School Educators. Kuykendall was appointed by President Carter as a chairperson of the National Advisory Council on Continuing Education. She has been in great demand as a speaker and presenter and has participated in more than 50 national conferences and dozens of state and local conferences across the U.S. She has also been a consultant to the U.S. Department of Defense Overseas Schools and has provided consulting services in Africa, Europe, and Australia. Perhaps her greatest asset in preparing this publication is her tremendous love of children and her belief in the humanity, goodness, and abilities of educators everywhere.

# DEDICATION

To the memories of my mother and husband, the unrelenting devotion of my father, and my extended family, my children, who continue to be the "wind beneath my wings," and countless professionals who have inspired me. This book also is dedicated to the children who will reap the ultimate benefits of this writing and to the individuals who will make those benefits possible.

# ACKNOWLEDGEMENTS

I wish to offer a special thanks to the individuals who provided the support and insight that allowed me to develop this publication. I could not have completed this work without their unconditional encouragement, inspirational spirit, and highly revered knowledge and understanding. They include Carlene Campbell, Cheryl Clark, Renee Grant, Billie Gray, Felice Kaufman, Keisha Kuykendall, Rasheki Kuykendall, Leonard McCants, Linda McCaskill, Vonetta McGee, and Shirlen Triplett.

# TABLE OF CONTENTS

# LIST OF TABLES AND WORKSHEETS

# PREFACE

When asked by the publisher to write this book, I became excited, but somewhat apprehensive. Certainly, I knew I had a lot to say. I remember so vividly the unbelievable joy and some of the early frustrations I experienced as a classroom teacher. I taught primary, junior and senior high school students, the majority of whom were Black, Hispanic, and very poor. I have come to know, firsthand, the tremendous capacity of every teacher to touch a life in a truly inspiring way.

Through my extensive travels around this country I have observed classes, teachers, and schools. I continue to hold the highest regard for educators who give so much of themselves on a daily basis. Yet, as special as teachers are, many have also known some very real frustrations. This book is intended to augment the joy and minimize the frustrations which are likely to surface when Black and Hispanic students are not reaching their full academic potential.

In writing this book, I knew I had a unique opportunity to share a perspective and some strategies that could assure the school success of many Black and Hispanic students. Yet, I also knew that this book could only have optimum impact if read with an open mind by committed individuals who also shared my love for childern and a concern for the betterment of society. I wanted to write a book which would inform, inspire, provoke, and replenish.

Hopefully, those who read these pages will see themselves as key players in the ongoing quest for school improvement.

Whether you are a school official, parent, student, or concerned citizen, you are crucial to the development of children and the creation of a more productive society. Not only do I want you to read this book, I want you to ask colleagues, friends, and family members to make use of the information and strategies shared.

Those who read these pages seeking additional insight, information, and teaching techniques will find them. The first three chapters lay a foundation for the implementation of the suggested activities and strategies presented in chapters four, five, six, and seven. While there is discussion in the early chapters of some of the issues that impact on individual and institutional change, there is also much encouragement for those most desirous of continued personal/professional growth and greater school success. The last two chapters provide some final thoughts for the future and an opportunity for personal assessment.

As you read, you'll notice that the words Black, Hispanic, and White are capitalized. In my opinion, these words define racial groups and should be upper case. I hope educators have both the pride and the persistence to facilitate school and life success for many diverse students.

If this book actually facilitates more school improvement—if only one more child is turned around by a teacher who was inspired as a result of this publication, then this endeavor was not in vain. I am indeed grateful for the opportunity to share.

# INTRODUCTION

*You must be your brother's keeper or he'll drag you down in his ruins.*

W.E.B. Dubois, 1907

Most Americans will readily attest to this nation's tremendous advances in technology and prosperity through the years. Even during periods of economic decline, many Americans could still acknowledge, appreciate, and share the pride of being part of a nation recognized as a dominant superpower. Through a study of history and a preoccupation with current world events, we have learned and been reminded of our ability as a nation to overcome obstacles and bask in the fulfillment of hard-won victories. As proud a nation as we are, however, and with as rich a history of struggle as we possess, as significant our numerous accomplishments, we are, in fact, a nation in grave jeopardy.

Some might even suggest that we are in danger of losing our capacity to care, and our propensity to provide the most fundamental opportunities to all of our children. It is the growing diversity of that population that has perhaps, ironically, stymied our ability to grow in humanity.

By the year 2020, the U.S. population will be 30% Black and Hispanic (U.S. Census Bureau, 1990). Several states will have "minority" populations that are, in fact, the majority. Black and Hispanic youth are already the majority population in dozens of urban school systems. By the year 2000, 42% of *all public school students* will come from these racial "minorities," and many will live in poverty (U.S. Bureau of Census,

1986). The changing demographics of our cities, suburbs, small towns, and rural areas will affect all of us in the years to come. The increasing diversity of our school population will have serious implications for our individual and collective survival.

The schools are not serving our Black and Hispanic youth well. Standardized test scores reflect these disparities. Data on suspensions, expulsions, retentions, and dropout rates indicate that far too many Black and Hispanic youth are being "distanced" from mainstream America. The continued underachievement and isolation of such a large and growing population is nothing short of a national tragedy. Unless more resources are put into the resolution of this crisis, the U.S. will remain a "Nation at Risk." Black youth are being buffeted by a series of forces that, if allowed to go unchecked, could create a "lost generation" (National Urban League, 1986, 1989, 1992). Yet, if this generation is lost, much of our hope for economic, social, and technological survival is also lost. The problem of educating these students must be addressed, or the consequences will be shared by each of us. Consider some of these troubling findings regarding Black youth:

- During the last decade, the proportion of Black men attending college suffered the largest decline of all racial and gender groups (American Council on Education/Education Commission of the States, 1988).

- The national dropout rate for all students continues to average between 17-19% but has been as high as 49.6% among Black youth in the last decade (Time Magazine, 1986).

- One out of every four Black men between the ages of 20 and 29 and one out of every eight Hispanic men of the same age is either in jail, on trial, or on parole (U.S. Department of Justice, 1991).

- The leading cause of death among 18- to 24-year-old Black men is murder by other Blacks (National Urban League, 1992).

- The fastest-growing homicide population is Black males between the ages of 11 and 22 (National Urban League, 1989).

- The largest increases in poverty are among Blacks without a college education (Center on Budget and Policy Priorities, 1988).

- More than two-thirds of all Black children in female-headed households are poor. For those children in homes where the Black mother is under 25 years of age, the poverty rate is 90% (National Urban League, the State of Black America, 1989).

- Black and Hispanic youth are suspended from schools at a rate three times that of their White counterparts (U.S. Department of Education, 1986).

According to the National Council of La Raza (NCLR), the future for Hispanic Youth is even more bleak. In its 1991 "State of Hispanic America" report, the NCLR compiled these distressing statistics:

- Hispanics are less likely than other racial or ethnic groups in this country to complete high school and less likely to have health insurance.

- Hispanics are more likely than Blacks to be segregated in inner city schools.

- The median earnings for Hispanic men are less than two-thirds the figure for non-Hispanic men—$14,141 compared to $22,207.

- More than 20% of Hispanic married couples are poor.

While these statistics are enough cause for alarm, there are some other disturbing trends which aren't as easily documented. Many school administrators take pride in having relatively low student dropout rates among Black and Hispanic students. Yet, the mere completion of high school by these youth does not solve the problem. The sad reality is that too many students are still receiving high school diplomas without the requisite motivation to lead enriching and productive lives. Even with high school diploma in hand, many still lack the hope and motivation to achieve lifelong success. Many more go through high school without ever believing they can really make it "legitimately" in a society they feel is against them.

Whether we are losing our youth "physically" through persistent dropout and expulsion trends or whether we are losing them mentally and emotionally, the bottom line is still the same. When they become convinced that they will not succeed academically, when they become convinced that they will not make it in "mainstream" America as a result of academic underachievement, they take whatever skills and ingenuity they *think* they possess and seek the "low" road of life. Without the skills and motivation necessary for legitimate prosperity, even high school graduates are likely to turn to unproductive pursuits—becoming easy prey to those who would enlist them in criminal and even violent activity. The challenge for educators is to help more of these youth make it to that "high road" of life.

Without a doubt, the education of Black and Hispanic youth must become a national priority. Educators have the greatest opportunity to motivate those students to achieve success in school and in life. Despite the nature of this challenge, educators—and especially teachers—must not lose hope. The research of Edmonds and others (1979) proves that despite the influences of the home and community, schools can have a positive impact on the achievement of youth. Although a negative teacher can discourage student development, an effective teacher can overcome the negative impact of prior conditioning (Mitchell & Conn, 1985).

Consider the fact that children, on average, spend approximately 6 hours a day in our schools. By the time they finish high school, they have spent an estimated 15,000 hours in school. Many will interact more with their "school family" (mostly teachers) than they will interact with their "families" at home—Monday through Friday. Through an understanding of the link between motivation and learning, teachers have a fantastic opportunity to make the best use of the time they have with their students.

This book was written to offer suggestions to those educators who have the interest, intent, and inspiration—but who may lack the information or teaching techniques—to facilitate the achievement motivation of Black and Hispanic students. It was also written to provide some strategies to allow other teachers to capture—and in most cases "recapture"—the *real joy of this great profession.*

Teachers have both the power and the presence to motivate students. An effective teacher can give a child, especially Black or Hispanic child, something many of their parents may be unable to give them: HOPE. With hope, there is reason to look to tomorrow. Without hope, life is meaningless. Without hope, there is greater propensity for negative behavior. When young people lose hope, they often wind up with an excess of another emotion—RAGE.

There is a growing rage among many of our youth. This "rage" among hopeless youth has caused many of us to live in fear and apprehension. Yet, this rage, and the dearth of hope which precedes it, can be diminished. We, as a nation, have a chance. We, as educators, have a chance to recapture the ultimate joy our profession can—and *must* provide. We can make life more meaningful by motivating all students to excel as never before.

The barriers to school success which confront so many Black and Hispanic students *can be eliminated.* Educators have such great opportunities to enrich the lives of "hopeless" children. Their education should be the concern of all of us—

policymakers, parents, politicians, businesspeople, and citizens in all walks of life. Teachers are *pivotal* players in society's quest to create a well-educated labor force and a more secure and prosperous citizenry. The efforts of caring educators can turn the tide and prevent the tragic and inevitable consequences which will beset this nation, and each one of us, if we lose any more of our youth to that "low road" of life.

*From Rage to Hope: Strategies for Reclaiming Black & Hispanic Youth* is intended to provide information, provoke thought, and replenish those educators willing to recommit to a rigorous but rewarding approach to the academic achievement of Black and Hispanic youth. It is offered as another resource for those exemplary educators seeking to add to their repertoire of techniques. The ideas in this book will help educators to:

- develop a greater appreciation of cultural diversity and differences among students.

- develop an understanding of how teacher expectations are formed and how they often contribute to student failure.

- strengthen the social and academic self-image of Black and Hispanic youth.

- overcome some of the school-related obstacles to long-term student success.

- learn more about motivating and monitoring the progress of Black and Hispanic youth.

- assess the performance and ability of diverse students more accurately.

- discipline students more effectively and creatively.

- create the most appropriate school and class climate.

- strengthen the home-school and school-community bonds.

The worksheets in Chapter Nine will help you assess your attitudes and behaviors, as well as those of your students. That knowledge, and the strategies offered in the text, provide the tools you can use to derive more professional satisfaction, reclaim Black and Hispanic students, and thus help shape America's future.

# 1  DEALING WITH DIFFERENCES

*There is no one Model American.*

American Association of
Colleges for Teacher Education, 1973

*I long for the day when we will be judged not by the color of our skins but by the content of our character.*

Rev. Dr. Martin Luther King, 1963

We all are products of our own cultures. We see people and things in the way we were conditioned to see them. All too often, innocently and inadvertently, we draw conclusions about others based on our own limited cultural perspectives. For example, a teacher raised believing that people who wear glasses are smarter than those who don't, would, inadvertently, engage in behavior which would reveal to her students those feelings and beliefs. Similarly, a teacher raised to believe that an "only child" is more likely to be a "loner" and underachiever than a child born of a large family is likely to make inferences and behavioral choices which reflect that belief.

The biggest challenge we face as educators is the challenge of stepping outside of our own cultural orientation so that we can develop a greater appreciation for and understanding of those who are different. We must be able to embrace the use of differing teaching techniques and strategies that reflect our appreciation of cultural diversity.

Despite the continued growth of diversity among Americans, there is still evidence that some people are unable to appreciate differences in others. Unequal treatment of different and diverse students in some of our educational institutions still exists in many areas, in spite of a long-term preoccupation with educational equality. The seeming disdain of some for diversity and the commensurate low tolerance for differences are reflected in some of the books and content regularly taught in many classrooms, the role models most commonly presented to students, the way students are treated in classroom interactions, and the assignment of certain students to particular instructional programs.[1] Blacks are still being portrayed as passive, docile, dependent, unenterprising, inferior and physically less attractive than Whites. In addition, the message was transmitted—through instruction— that "all a racial minority had to do to succeed was to adopt the requisite culture of the dominant society."[2] Children were taught to emulate and pay tribute to those who conformed to middle-class mainstream cultural standards of heroism. Individuals whose heroism involved fighting oppression, preserving cultural integrity, or combating social injustices in ways that were not sanctioned by mainstream culture were not to be lauded or, in most instances, even discussed in the curriculum.[3] Many educators still respond to students who are different in predictable ways—they isolate them, ignore them, retain them, suspend them, and in far too many instances, simply fail to instruct them.

Considering the continued high rates of tracking, ability grouping, suspension, and low level instruction for Black and Hispanic students, we must again ask ourselves, "What is our purpose in teaching? How far are we willing to go in providing diverse youth with the motivation and skills they will need for success in a technocratic society?" Each educator will have to answer this question. However, each educator also must understand how the inability to deal with student differences can impact classroom performance.

## Teacher Attitudes

Teacher attitudes have consequences. Once teachers develop low expectations, and the accompanying negative behavior, they send signals that suggest the student is hopeless. In a study of multicultural high school dropouts in 1982, students described their teachers as "unhappy with their jobs, disgruntled, bored, boring, unfair, and sometimes humiliating."[4] A similar study of teacher behavior on the attitudes of urban youth concluded that one of the biggest problems in educating these youth was changing the behavior of teachers who often erode student confidence and their fragile sense of acceptance of their peers. Students were likely to go to great lengths to avoid teachers who they felt had placed them in uncomfortable and humiliating positions.[5] All too often, there is then a reluctance on the teacher's part to use educational programs or teaching techniques that will yield positive outcomes and enhance student motivation.[6]

Obviously, the reverse is also true. An effective teacher generally has an attitude brimming with confidence and encouragement. With the right attitude, with a fond appreciaton of the individuality, uniqueness, and ability of every student, a teacher can ensure student success. Without such an attitude, there's a dearth of effort, a loss of hope, and an acceptance of student failure.

Those student differences most likely to impact on teacher attitudes and expectations are the following:

- prior student achievement.
- prior student behavior.
- prior student placement.
- socioeconomic status.
- language ability.
- physical attraction.
- gender.
- race/ethnicity.

A brief discussion of these critical areas of difference is necessary.

***Prior student achievement***. There have been numerous studies on the impact of prior student achievement on teacher attitudes and expectations. In assessing teacher evaluations of students, Murray, Herling, and Staebler found that teachers are influenced by the initial performance of their students.[7] There is even evidence that some Black children receive lower grades than White children even when they have the identical academic performance.[8]

Although most educators know that students learn and grow at different rates, many educators still have expectations that all students will develop academic competencies at or about the same time. Children are often penalized for a slow academic start. Many of these children lose the belief that they will ever achieve skill mastery. It's important that all educators accept differences in growth and development. Such acceptance, however, should not discourage efforts to enhance student achievement. For example, few educators are likely to show indifference to children who are physically bigger or smaller than other children their age. Educators often accept the fact that boys are likely to develop gross motor skills faster than girls, but many educators develop lower expectations when boys fail to develop fine motor skills at the same pace of their female counterparts.

Children come into "their own" at differing ages. Some mature emotionally before others their same age, and others develop certain academic and non-academic skills before their peers. Too much emphasis is being placed on facilitating simultaneous achievement gains. Children who are unfortunate enough to develop responsibility and understanding later in their childhood—or adolescence—are at a regrettable disadvantage. All too often decisions are made about a child's curriculum and school success based on how *fast* a child learned in kindergarten or the primary grades.

Such emphasis on differing academic competencies among primary children is not only unfair, but dangerous. Many students come from homes where parents are unaware that they should teach their children how to read and write *before* they start kindergarten. Many parents have been socialized to believe that it is up to the schools to develop the academic skills and motivation in their children. The difference in expectations of what a child should know *before* starting school is one reason so many youth are being labeled "slow" before they've had a chance to demonstrate their learning potential.

Prior achievement may also be stymied when a child is in a learning environment where there is an incongruence between his or her learning style and the teacher's teaching style. Learning style differences may not affect *ability*, but they do affect *performance*.

***Prior student behavior.*** Not only are many youth penalized for their lack of prior knowledge (as opposed to their lack of ability), many Black and Hispanic youth are penalized for not knowing how to "behave" in school or for exhibiting behavior that is too different from that of their White counterparts. Behavioral problems of many Black and Hispanic youth often reflect cultural differences. Cultural conflict and behavioral problems are more likely to emerge when these youth are unaware of expected cultural or communicative norms. Quite often, when the school's cultural or communicative norms are violated, it is considered an act of defiance. Despite the intentions of the students, decisions are made about their behavior based on the interpretation and perspective of those in authority positions within the schools.

For example, many Black children are enthusiastic and assertive in school when they are required to be passive and non-expressive. Some teachers are likely to react to this enthusiasm by engaging in negative dominant behavior, thereby limiting the mobility, action, exuberance, and motivation of children who thrive on movement and excitement. Such labels as "hyperactive" or "behavioral disorders" often are given to these students, even though their in-school behavior merely reflects their out-of-school socialization.

While there are rules and procedures that must be followed, too many teachers have established as their *priority* the maintenance of "order" in the classroom. This means that children who are naturally quiet, docile, and unexciting have an advantage. Those children who question and challenge teachers or who display emotional swings are often psychoanalyzed and, worse, disciplined to the point that they no longer want to be in our classrooms or to be productive members of our society.

Students who have previously made mistakes in judgment or behavior are often dealt with unfairly from then on. A survey of counselors in several urban school districts revealed that decisions often are made about guilt in student infractions based on previous student behavior.[9] A student who has improved his or her behavior is unlikely to get the benefit of the doubt in many schools. Teachers must remember that every child has a right to be judged based on current situations and circumstances, not on previous mistakes.

***Prior student placement.*** Much has been written and said about the negative impact of tracking, ability grouping, and use of student labels. As early as 1968, experts were documenting the powerful impact of labels and placements on diminishing expectations. Rosenthal & Jacobson found that when teachers were told that randomly selected students were gifted, intellectually blooming high achievers, teachers responded with behavior that had a significant positive impact on student motivation, actual classroom performance, and achievement on standardized tests.[10]

Many educators react to children who are different by placing them in low-achievement ability groups and low tracks. One study found that Black children are three times more likely than their White counterparts to be identified as educable mentally retarded and only one-third as likely to be identified and placed with the gifted and talented.[11] All too often, Black and Hispanic youth are placed in low-level tracks, ability groups, and special education classrooms when they fail to show mastery of the mainstream culture, when they show a disrespect for school authority, when they lack "self-control" or an interest in course content, or when they fail to get along with the teacher and other classmates.

Many of the placements and labels for Black and Hispanic youth are grossly unfair. Some who are labeled as having "B.D." (behavioral disorder), for example, are simply exhibiting a negative response to a teacher they feel is unfair. Other students (especially primary children) may be unaware that excessive energy, enthusiasm, and excitement are disallowed in many classrooms.

The "LD" label also has been overused. While there are children with "learning disabilities," the reality is that many of the Black and Hispanic youth who seem "disabled" simply *learn differently* and must be taught differently if they are to succeed. If a teacher already harbors a negative attitude about a particular culture or race, the placement of a racially or culturally different child in a special education class or low-ability track will only diminish the expectations of that teacher, thereby exacerbating the problem and limiting the chances of school success for that student.[12]

***Socioeconomic status.*** During the 1970s there was a great deal of research on the impact of social class on teacher expectations. Decisions about student potential, ability, and performance often were based on family income and status.[13] By 1978 it was widely accepted that the socioeconomic basis for teacher expectations was a contributing factor to the inability of schools to make an impact on students independent of background and general social context.[14]

Ron Edmonds and the Effective Schools research indicate that schools can enhance student achievement *regardless of home influences or socioeconomic status.* Yet, there is evidence that many educators, administrators, and policy makers still view class and family status/income as indices of student potential. The use of such negative descriptors as "economically disadvantaged," "culturally deprived," and "under-privileged" indicates the existence of some distorted attitudes and perceptions regarding the likelihood of success for children of poverty. I can speak from personal experience on the need to move away from such damaging terminology.

Recently, in a mixed audience of educators and counselors, a teacher complimented me on my obvious academic and professional success. She observed "You are a true American success." "But," she added, "many of us don't get students like you. I'm sure you'll have to admit that you made it, you succeeded in school and in later life because of your *home influence and the example set by your parents.* Don't you have to admit that you made it, more than anything else, because of that home influence and the foundation for success laid by your parents?" My answer shocked her. While I am fortunate to have been blessed with two wonderful and loving parents, the reality is:

- I was born to an unwed 19-year-old high school graduate who would later become a school crossing guard for 30 years.

- I was born on a kitchen table in low-income 2-story housing projects (The Brooks Projects) on the west side of Chicago.

- My father was a 7th-grade dropout who was later honorably discharged from World War II because of numerous injuries that make him a "disabled veteran." He is physically unable to work and has lived for all of *my life on government stipends due to his war injuries.*

- My father was so embarrassed by our poverty, he never even visited the school (except for graduations). By the time I reached adulthood, I sought the reason for his lack of visibility. He explained he stayed away for "fear of embarrassing" me.

- We were poor and everyone in the neighborhood was poor but we discovered early that, for us, Black LOVE was truly Black wealth.

- When my mother succumbed to heart failure and an untimely death at the age of 56, her *only* material possessions were those I bought for her during my adulthood.

- I never had parents who could help with homework, do science projects for me, or tutor me to do well on the California Achievements, Iowa Basics, SAT, or ACT, or other exams. They honestly believed that my teachers would give me all of the love and support needed to excel in school. They were right.

I consider myself *very fortunate.* I was educated in poor neighborhoods on the west and south sides of Chicago by teachers willing to do whatever was deemed necessary to bring out the best in this poor black girl. I was especially fortunate to have teachers who were patient, committed, and encouraging. Despite a very slow start, I was convinced by caring and nurturing educators that I was quite capable of academic and lifelong success. I am eternally grateful to those teachers who took the time to mold and motivate.

Perhaps I'm also lucky that I didn't find out until I got to college (on four academic scholarships) that I was "culturally deprived," "economically disadvantaged," and "underprivileged." I only discovered recently that in addition, I was also "at-risk," "latch-key" and even came from what now would be referred to as a "dysfunctional" family. I was like so many Black and Hispanic youth in our schools today. While others may refer to it as a "horrid childhood," few will understand how truly happy I really was.

Many teachers will find more gratification when they are able to look past the labels that are affixed to children of poverty. The cycle of poverty that exists in many families can be broken. In their endeavors to inspire and give "hope," educators cannot only help to break such cycles of poverty, they can strengthen the human resolve of many poor students for personal excellence. However, educators will not succeed until they accept, understand, and build on the untapped learning potential of every low-income child.

*Language ability.* In her research on Teacher Expectations, Sheryl Denbo found evidence of biases based on language differences.[15] Children who speak standard English are expected to perform better academically than those students who use non-standard English.[16] Even in situations where Black and Chicano students had speech performance equal to or better than that of White students, teachers still "heard" them as inferior.[17]

Many Black and Hispanic youth are likely to start school clinging to the language of their homes, the language of the streets, or the language of their own subculture. Teachers can still show appreciation of different dialects. Teacher who give the impression of racial or cultural superiority only foster the development of an "us *versus them*" mentality in many Black or Hispanic youth. This mentality and subsequent alienation only increase if allowed to go unchecked.

Williams, Whitehead, and Miller have argued that

> ...given the relationship between language attitudes and teacher expectancy, there is the suggestion that with the study of language variations in children, particularly 'minority' group children, attitudinal correlates be introduced into the curricula of teacher training to prevent language attitudes from serving as false prophecies, or worse yet, becoming themselves self-fulfilled prophecies.[18]

In a society as diverse as ours, language differences are going to exist. Every American is a product of his or her culture. The first language spoken by all of us was the language of the home. One who speaks with an accent was probably born into a home where others spoke with the same accent. If born into a home where the English spoken is non-standard, broken, "Black," or non-existent, a child will learn to speak in that dialect. This does not mean that students who are unable to speak standard English cannot succeed academically. This also does not mean that children cannot or should not be taught standard English. It simply means that teachers must not denigrate the language of the child's culture.

***Physical attraction.*** Unfortunately, ours has become a society where "good looks" are highly revered. Students deemed unattractive are often ridiculed, even by their teachers. A study of fifth-grade teachers found that a child's attractiveness was significantly associated with the teacher's expectations concerning the child's intelligence, his or her parents' interest in education, the likelihood of future success, and popularity with peers.[19] While there are numerous teachers who do not judge students based on how they look, dress, or even smell, a significant number still do. In my own personal observations and informal discussions with teachers around the nation, I am appalled by the frequent negative reference to FLK's "funny looking kids," particularly with regard to Black and Hispanic youth.

This inability of some teachers to see beauty in *every* child does carry implications for the education and motivation of Black and Hispanic students. There are some Black and Hispanic youth who are likely to see themselves as unattractive, based on White standards of beauty. Student perceptions of their attractiveness affect self-image. Many young girls often turn to teen pregnancy and unsafe (and even *deadly*) sex, just to find someone to love them for who they really are. Educators can augment student self-worth, dignity, and self-love by making students feel that they are beautiful—inside and out.

***Gender.*** It is not unusual for teachers to express preferences for male or female students. The very existence of Title IX of the Elementary and Secondary Education Act of 1965 suggests a propensity of educators to treat students unequally based on gender. The current preoccupation by many with the crisis of Black and Hispanic male children is further indication that these males are not receiving equal or, in some cases, even fair treatment in our schools. Gender bias among some teachers still accounts for diminishing teacher expectations and the poor implementation of effective teaching strategies.

Since the late 1980s, programs have been initiated in some urban cities—Detroit, Michigan, and Baltimore, Maryland, are prime examples—to separate Black male students and to create "all Black male" classes with Black male teachers who can serve as exemplary role models. The intent was to decrease the widening gap in the achievement and dropout rates between Black male and Black female students. Many experts feel this widening disparity was partly a result of gender bias. Some Black educators have even alluded to a national conspiracy to destroy Black boys.[20] Whether one chooses to accept the conspiracy theory or not, few can deny that gender bias still exists in some places. There is still a misconception held by many citizens about the abilities, attitudes, and proclivities for violence of Black and Hispanic males.

*Race.* This is also a very serious indicator of bias. The research on the impact of a student's race on teacher expectations and behavior is abundant. Some teachers continue to hold lower expectations of Black and Hispanic youth and reveal these expectations by giving less praise, encouragement, attention, and interest to these youths.[21]

The issue of race is still pervasive in America and is likely to continue to be as we move into the year 2000. Each teacher will have to assess his or her own feelings about students who are racially or culturally different. Many educators still see the education of Black and Hispanic children to be a major challenge. However, the challenge need not be overwhelming. There are many committed educators, but there is a need for even more commitment, sensitivity, and understanding of the academic needs, learning style preferences and abilities of racially diverse students so that greater numbers of teachers can implement appropriate strategies for improved achievement in Black and Hispanic students.

Teachers can reverse the consequences of low expectations by avoiding these behaviors. In Table III, other tips for giving supportive feedback are:

1.  Children respond better when eye contact is direct, sincere, loving, and encouraging.

2.  Children are more likely to modify behavior when comments are directed at specific behavior, rather than general actions. For example, children are likely to feel worse when they are told they have "misbehaved" than when they are told what specific action caused a teacher to think they were disobedient. When possible, the child should be talked to privately.

3.  Children also respond better when a teacher's comments are descriptive rather than evaluative. By describing their own reactions as opposed to the student's behavior, teachers are more likely to be seen as supportive rather than judgmental.

4.  Children must feel a teacher is taking into account their needs; therefore, a teacher's comments should reflect genuine concern for the child's needs as well as those of the teacher.

5.  Comments are most effective when timed close to the behavior. Children are unlikely to remember feedback that is given long after the action or assignment is completed.

6.  By checking with individual students, sometimes privately, teachers can make sure their comments and feelings are understood.

Once teachers can deal effectively with student differences, they can augment and strengthen the academic self-image and motivation so vital to life-long success. In order to make sure you're not missing an opportunity to motivate a student, ask yourself these questions:

1.  Have you developed a more positive attitude about the potential of diverse students?

2.  Are you convinced that you can enhance the confidence of children who have had a slow start?

3.  Is the *achievement of all students* your main priority?

4.  Are you willing to explore proven alternatives to tracking and ability grouping?

5.  Are you willing to refrain from using stereotypical and negative labels?

6.  Can you teach students to speak and write standard English while accepting their cultural dialect as another legitimate form of expression?

7.  Can you look past physical attraction, gender, and race to find the untapped potential in your students?

8.  Can you help colleagues in your school or district respond to diversity and student differences in a more positive manner?

If you answered "yes" to all of those questions, you'll find it easier to enhance the self-image of all students and to make effective use of the suggested activities which appear in later chapters.

# Notes

1.  Sadler, M. and D. & Long, L., "Gender and Educational Equality." In Banks, J. and C.A., eds., *Multicultural Education-Issues and Perspectives.* (Boston: Allyn and Bacon, 1989).

2.  Dickerman, M., "Teaching Cultural Pluralism" in Banks, J. *Teaching Ethnic Studies.* Taken from Gay, G. "Achieving Educational Equality through Curriculum Desegregation." *Phi Delta Kappan*, Sept. 1990.

3.  Ibid.

4.  Olsen, G. and More, M. *Voices From The Classroom Oakland*, CA: Citizens Policy Center, 1982.

5.  Fine, M. "Why Urban Adolescents Drop Into and Out of Public High Schools." *Teachers College Board*, Spring 1986.

6.  Cooper, H. M., et. al. "Understanding Pygmalion: The Social Psychology of Self-Fulfilling Classroom Expectations." Alexandria VA ERIC Document Reproduction Service, ED 182 642, 1979.

7.  Murray, H.B., Herling, B.B., and Staebler, B.K. "The Effects of Locus of Control and Pattern of Performance on Teacher Evaluation of a Student." *Psychology in the Schools* 10 1973:345-50.

8.  Robovits, P.C. and Maehr, M.L. "Pygmalion in Black and White." *Journal of Personality and Social Psychology*, 25 February 1973.

9.  Kuykendall, C. "Survey of Urban School Counselor Attitudes on Disruptive Students." 1984-1986.

10. Rosenthal, R., and Jacobson, L. *Pygmalion in the Classroom: Teacher Expectations and Pupils Intellectual Development*. New York: Holt, Rinehart and Winston, 1968, taken from Denbo, Sheryl, *Improving Multicultural Student Achievement: Focus on the Classroom* Wash., D.C. 1986.

11. Childrens Defense Fund. *Black and White Children in America: Key Facts*. Washington, D.C. Childrens Defense Fund, 1985.

12. Fair, G.W. "Coping with Double-Barrelled Discrimination." *Journal of School Health* 50 May 1980.

13. Cooper, H.M., Baron, R.M., and Louie, C.A. "The Importance of Race and Social Class Information in the Formation of Expectancies About Academic Performance." *Journal of Education Psychology* 67 1975.

14. Gollub, W.L., and Sloan, E. "Teacher Expectations and Race and Socioeconomic Status." *Urban Education* 13 1978.

15. Denbo, S. *Improving Multicultural Student Achievement: Focus On the Classroom*. Mid-Atlantic Center for Race Equity, American University, Wash., D.C. 1986.

16. Smith, R.P., and Denton, J.J. "The Effects of Dialect, Ethnicity and Orientation to Sociolinguistics on the Perception of Teaching Candidates." *Educational Research Quarterly* 3 Spring 1980.

17. Choy, S.J. and Dodd, D.H. "Standard-English-Speaking and Nonstandard Hawaiian on English-Speaking Children: Comprehension of Both Dialects and Teachers' Evaluations." *Journal of Educational Psychology* 68, April 1976.

18. Williams, F.; Whitehead, J.L.; and Miller, L. "Relations between Language Attitudes and Teacher Expectancy." *American Educational Research Journal* Spring 1972; Taken from Denbo, S. Op. Cit.

19. Clifford, M.M., and Walster, E. "Research Note: The Effect of Physical Attractiveness on Teacher Expectations." *Sociology of Education* 46, Spring 1973.

20. Kunjufu, J. *The Conspiracy to Destroy Black Boys' African-American Images*, Chicago, IL 1985.

21. Denbo, S. Op. Cit.

## 2 THE IMPACT OF STUDENT SELF-IMAGE ON ACHIEVEMENT AND MOTIVATION

*We cannot possibly bring out the best in our children
unless we're willing to give the best of ourselves...*

Crystal Kuykendall, 1989

Since the early 1960s, educators, parents, and psychologists have debated the impact of self-image on the achievement and motivation of children. The development of the self-images of Black and Hispanic students is especially significant if we are to prepare them for meaningful roles in mainstream America.

Youth form their self-image largely based on how they think they are being perceived by significant adults in their lives. Individuals must have a high self-image if they are to cope effectively with the demands of their lives. Imbedded in the self-image of children is the hope for all of our futures. Unless they feel secure and happy in the present, children are unable to think positively about the future.[1]

Studies of Head Start programs show improved achievements as a result of efforts to improve self-image.[2] Even a study of recruits in the armed forces provided evidence of the importance of self-image in the development of self-control. A study by Little in 1968 revealed that learning progress was attributed to opportunities for the development of self-image and the feeling of group participation.[3]

Self-image is enhanced by praise and acceptance and lowered by criticism and unwarranted disapproval. Although there is evidence that older children and teenagers base much of their self-image on the perceptions of their peers, research by Gilmore shows that this is due to the fact that these children reach out to peer groups as substitutes for a perceived lack of adult affection and turn to peers when their self-image needs are not met by adults.[4] It is the *development of a child's self-image* that is perhaps the most important barometer in assessing probability of future success.

Self-image is shaped and molded over and over again by an individual's life experiences. The building of self-image requires constant renewal and reinforcement as long as the individual lives. Affection and love are the lifeblood of emotional growth. The small child loses self-esteem when she or he perceives the loss of love and attains it when she or he regains love.[5] Self-image is molded as children derive satisfaction from their ability to do well at something.

Teachers, schools, parents, peers, and significant others have a critical role to play in the development of self-image in Black and Hispanic youth.

Children develop two self-images as they mature into adulthood: a "social self-image" and an "academic self-image." The distinctions between the two are significant.

## The Social Self-Image

The social self-image is very often the self-image of the home, the self-image of the playground, the self-image of the streets, the basketball court, the football field, etc. The social self-image can be described in relation to others who are a part of the social environment. The social self-image determines most often how individuals feel about their interaction with others. It is reflected in how individuals carry themselves, how they speak, how they adorn themselves, how they react in social settings, and how they develop social skills.

There are three primary influences in the development of the social self-image in Black and Hispanic students: the home and family, the peer group, and other social systems.

***Role of the home and family in shaping the social self-image.*** Parents, siblings, and other family members have much to do with how a child internalizes feelings of love and acceptance. Social skills, personality, and character are shaped in the formative years before school by the family. Similarly, a child's perception of his or her physical attraction and non-academic abilities are molded in these early years as a result of the influences of those within the family circle.

Children who have strong bonds with members of their "family unit"—regardless of family size, income, or status—are likely to see themselves in the most positive light. On the other hand, children who experience aloofness, excessive criticism, and lack of love within the family circle are likely to fault themselves. Even sibling rivalry can be damaging to the development of a strong social self-image in some children.

***Role of the peer group in shaping the social self-image.*** Black and Hispanic youth are like all humans; they require acceptance. They are likely to be especially loyal to those who show an acceptance of shortcomings, an appreciation of their strengths, and an approval of their unique talents and abilities. Alvin Poussaint, a renowned Black psychologist, found that Black children have strong needs for achievement and approval.[6] Very often, these needs are satisfied in peer groups where rapport is established and bonds are made. In a comparative study of self-perceptions among Black girls and boys, Bruce Hare found that the self-image of Black boys depended on non-academic factors such as social ability and peer acceptance. The self-image of Black girls, in comparison, was related more strongly to academic achievement.[7]

It is through the acceptance of the peer group that many youth develop behavioral norms. The way many Black youth talk, walk, dress, dance, play competitive sports, rap, and even "play the dozens"* with one another reflects the extent to which they have internalized their self-worth and "place" within their peer group subculture. How they see themselves in the context of peer relations is very important to their social development. When peers provide appreciation and approval, they often become the primary support unit.

***Role of the other social systems in shaping the social self-image.*** Within the Black community, there are significant social systems, such as the Black church, boys/girls clubs, and structured and unstructured recreation centers. Many Black youth who are given significant roles to play in the Black church (e.g., through membership in church organizations and participation in skits, plays, and other church events) develop strong bonds and a positive social self-image. Similarly, Hispanic youth who bond with adult community figures through organized recreational and social activities where their self-worth is proclaimed, are also likely to develop strong social self-images.

Many Black and Hispanic youth benefit greatly from these community, peer, and family bonds when the relationships are positive. Even when the relationships lead to negative behavior (as in violent gangs), the strong social self-image

---

* NOTE: Playing the "dozens" (also called "jonin" or "signifyin") is an art in most Black communities because it requires emotional control, creative thinking, mental agility and quickness, and a sense of humor. It usually involves two males in a verbal "showdown" where both take turns in making negative and derogatory statements—which most often are not intended to show disrespect—about each other or some member of the other person's family—often the mother (example: "Your mother is so fat that when she jumped in the air she got stuck"). The "dozens" is usually played before an audience of peers, who laugh and express some indication of who they think is "winning". Even though there are rare instances where the two players may resort to fighting, most see it as a playful "duel" where they can show off a skill and avoid physical contact. Even when youth are aggressive and loud when playing the "dozens," teachers should understand it does not necessarily mean they are preparing for a fight. Certainly, students should not be disciplined unfairly for engaging in this ritual.

is likely to be left intact as the desire for appreciation, loyalty, and support is nurtured.

## The Academic Self-Image

As powerful as the social self-image is, it alone does not indicate the likelihood for future success in a high-tech society. Nor does it determine the extent to which youth are likely to be motivated to achieve success in "mainstream America." It is the academic self-image that dictates how well children will fare in a society where survival will require higher-order thinking skills and other academic competencies. It is not unusual for some children to display a positive social self-image within their own families and communities and a negative academic self-image in educational environments.

The academic self-image is molded in our classrooms. Years ago Charles Silberman found that 80% of Black children have positive self-images when they enter school, 20% still do by the fifth grade, but only 5% do by their senior year in high school.[8] In a 1985 study of the progressively decreasing scores of Black students on Comprehensive Tests of Basic Skills in the District of Columbia Public Schools, Bell found that, as Black children mature, they begin to experience many hostilities imposed by the "majority" culture.[9] Such hostilities often are rooted in the inability of teachers to augment the academic self-image of these youth.

The key ingredient for improving the academic self-image of all youth is "accomplishment." An academic environment that offers encouragement, praise, and the opportunity for accomplishment will promote the development of a positive self-image.[10] Children who are without significant opportunities for in-school success are likely to feel frustrated and inept. However, since the need for accomplishment (of any kind) is so great, many students who are denied in-school success will seek accomplishment outside of school—even if it is through illegal or unacceptable behavior.

The academic self-image is unlikely to be enhanced when teachers provide an academic experience that is defeating and discouraging. Levin found that teachers who have negative attitudes toward their students contribute to the massive educational failure of Black children.[11] Yet, an attempt by teachers to build on the positive *social* strengths of Black and Hispanic youth can actually serve to enhance the *academic self-image.* Martin found the focus by teachers on student strengths made them feel more confident thereby enhancing a positive self-image.[12] Teachers can augment the academic self-image by identifying and developing some of the unique cultural and social strengths Black and Hispanic youth bring to the classroom. An understanding of how the social self-image can be used to bolster the academic self-image is critical.

Table I provides a partial listing of characteristics of low academic self-image and high social self-image which many Black youth, especially boys, are likely to display in tandem.[13]

**TABLE I**

**LOW ACADEMIC SELF-IMAGE AND HIGH SOCIAL SELF-IMAGE**

| Characteristics of *Low Academic Self-Image* | Characteristics of *High Social Self-Image* |
| --- | --- |
| Failure to complete work | Confidence in performing before others |
| Hostility/disruptive behavior or defiant speech in class | Unique ability in social skills such as sports, dancing, "playing the dozens," rapping, etc. |
| Daydreaming, poor attention span | Mutual supportive system with other peers |
| Little or no eye contact | Keen interest and preoccupation with social activities such as listening to music, dancing, sports participation, art work, etc. |
| Frequent use of excuses | Non-verbal communication and eye contact |
| Fear of failure and of trying | Persistence in the *learning* and performance of social skills (e.g., bike riding, card playing, music, sports, etc.) |

**TABLE I (continued)**

| Characteristics of<br>*Low Academic Self-Image* | Characteristics of<br>*High Social Self-Image* |
|---|---|
| Repeated and deliberate tardiness and absences | Desire for success in "social" functions/ notice of others |
| No volunteering or participating | Extensive desire for interaction with those most encouraging and supportive |
| Tendency to be withdrawn and isolated | Friendly, sincere behavior |
| Dislike for school and/or the school teacher | Facial expression and body movements reflect enjoyment |
| Facial expressions and body movement tend to show visible pain, frustration, and anxiety | Facial expressions and body movements reflect enjoyment |

(These responses are those provided most often by more than 2,000 teachers surveyed by Crystal Kuykendall between 1984-1987.)

Because the academic self-image of Black and Hispanic students is vital to their academic success, teachers must work hard to ensure that these students have positive experiences in school. Black youth may be taught at home to appreciate certain skills that are not always valued in classrooms and that do not reflect the school's norms. These include nonverbal communication, dance and rhythmic movements, learning through cooperation, and verbal interplay during instruction. They may also acquire social "survival" strategies similar to the behavior of others in their communities and culture (e.g., the "hip" walking styles, expressive movements, or use of "Black English"). This duality between the culture of the school and the culture of the family and community can account for much of the discrepancy between academic and social self-concept.

The indicators and characteristics of low academic self-image presented in Table I have been observed by many teachers and school officials. What is needed most, however, is an understanding of why these characteristics exist. The list below will provide more insight.[14]

1. *Children who fail to complete work*...often have either a fear of failure ("I won't get a passing grade anyway") or a fear of success. They consequently lack the desire to do well—usually because the need for approval will still go unmet. Some children may simply lack interest in the subject area.

2. *Children who are hostile, disruptive, delinquent, and/or defiant in speech in the presence of teachers*...actually have a "fear" of other people. Their hostility is part of a warped rationale—"do unto others before they get the chance to do unto you." These children have been mistreated and emotionally abused. They are often hostile as a means of protecting themselves from additional hurt. All too often, the "hurt" is exacerbated in a classroom that doesn't allow for an emphasis on strengths, or teachers who have negative expectations.

3. *Children who daydream or show a poor attention span*...are not motivated to succeed and in many cases are disinterested in what is being taught. They either think they are going to fail—even if they do pay attention—or are not inspired (by teachers, peers, or parents) to succeed. Some smaller children may be unaware of the importance of school and the need to pay attention.

4. *Children who have little or no eye contact*...may be socialized to feel direct eye contact is a sign of disrespect—particularly if the speaker is an adult. However, if no such cultural socialization is evident, little or no eye contact usually indicates a fear of people. Very often the child may not look adults in the eye because he sees "dislike" for him in the other person's eyes. When there is no real love, direct eye contact makes it more obvious. Many Black youth who are especially proficient in non-verbal communication will detect—or think they've detected—bias in their teacher's eyes, making eye contact with that teacher even more painful.

5. *Children who frequently use excuses to justify poor performance are afraid of what others (teachers) think of*

*them*...These children often need a crutch to justify what they fear most—failure. They have been made to feel inferior but are still fighting against what they perceive to be a teacher's negative impressions. In making excuses, they are actually trying to hold on to some semblance of dignity. This is merely an endeavor to save face, or to assuage their feelings of inadequacy.

6.  *Children who are afraid to try and who give up too easily*...generally have a fear of failure. They have already determined that the best way to prevent the pain of not doing well is to abstain from making the attempt. All too often, student confidence has not been built in one area of "strength" and the result is an unwillingness to try. Children who have a sense of purpose, who *feel* motivated, and who *know* others believe in them will eventually lose this characteristic. By the same token, children who "give up too easily"—who don't persist—also have a fear of failure. They lack the confidence to keep going because they really don't feel they *will* meet with success.

7.  *Children with repeated and deliberate tardiness or absences*...may have such a "fear of failure" or a "fear of people" that they will do anything to avoid being in a situation where embarrassment, pain, or failure is imminent. Cutting class or ditching school is one way to avoid the pain of being in unbearable situations. Some children are absent or tardy for reasons beyond their control; this analysis is not applicable to those youth who don't intentionally have poor attendance. Some children are tardy because of other extenuating circumstances. For example, an older child may be responsible for getting a younger sibling to class on time and may be unable to make it to his/her own class by the time the bell rings. Remember, also, that children are people too, and like most people, find it hard to be some place "on time" when their "souls" really *don't want to be there at all.*

8. *Children who don't volunteer or participate*...may fear failure or success. If they haven't been *motivated to succeed*, volunteering and participating are unattractive. If they fear ridicule for wrong answers or actions, volunteering is practically prohibitive. In addition, many Black and Hispanic youth don't volunteer if they don't feel a teacher *expects* (or wants) this of them.

9. *Children who tend to be withdrawn and isolated*...behave this way very often when not treated with respect and confidence. They have a fear of people and may find interaction with others, in what they perceive as a hostile school environment, threatening and painful. Disparities in class, race, and culture between student and teacher can create such feelings of isolation.

10. *Children who dislike school and/or the school teacher*...will eventually develop such a painful hostility for, or fear of, that teacher, that they withdraw from the learning process.

Educators who endeavor to motivate Black and Hispanic students must recognize that both the school environment and teacher behavior can contribute to either the development or the alleviation of these characteristics. Quite often, these characteristics indicate a fear of, or intimidation by, other people. Children experiencing this emotion may do things to give people a reason to dislike them. Often, however, they go to great extremes to win approval and affection. It is so important for teachers to understand that some children exhibiting these characteristics have been emotionally bruised. Sensitive to even the most unintentional slights, and well aware of the existence of racism, sexism, and classism, many of these youth are only seeking to prevent additional emotional pain.

The next chapter discusses some of the school-related obstacles to achievement that must be overcome. Chapter 4 offers a variety of strategies for removing these obstacles, and specific suggestions for motivating Black and Hispanic students in school.

## Notes

1.  Gilmore, J. and E. *Give Your Child A Future.* Englewood Cliffs, N.J.: Prentice-Hall, Inc., 1982.

2.  Lazar, I. and Darlington, R. *Summary: Lasting Effects After Pre-School.* Ithaca, N.Y.: Cornell University, 1978.

3.  Little, R. "Basic Education of Socialization in the Armed Forces" *American Journal of Orthopsychiatry,* October 1968.

4.  Gilmore, J. and E. Op. Cit.

5.  Ibid.

6.  Bell Jr., C. "Explaining the Progressively Decreasing Scores on Comprehensive Tests of Basic Skills (CTBS) of the School Children of the District of Columbia Public Schools as They Progress from Elementary School into High School." Alexandria, VA. ERIC Document Reproduction Service, ED 226 234, 1985.

7.  Hare, B. "Black Girls: A Comparative Analysis of Self-Perceptions and Achievement by Race, Sex and Socioeconomic Background." John Hopkins University, 1979.

8.  Silberman, C. *Crisis in the Classroom.* New York, N.Y.: Vintage Books, 1971.

9.  Bell, Jr., C. "Explaining the Progressively Decreasing Scores on Comprehensive Tests of Basic Skills (CTBS) of the School Children of the District of Columbia Public Schools as They Progress from Elementary School into High School." Alexandria, VA. ERIC Document Reproduction Service, ED 226 234, 1985.

10  Mitchell, W. and Conn, C.P. *Power of Positive Students.* New York, N.Y.: Morrow Publishing Co., 1985.

11. Levin, H.M. and Schutze, H., eds. *Financing Recurrent Education: Strategies for Improving Employment, Job Opportunities and Productivity.* Beverly Hills, CA: Sage Publications, 1983.

12. Martin, R. *Teaching Through Encouragement* Englewood Cliffs, New Jersey: Prentice Hall, Inc. 1980.

13. Kuykendall, C. *Improving Black Student Achievement by Enhancing Students' Self-Image.* Washington, D.C.: American University, 1989.

14. Ibid.

# 3 SCHOOL-RELATED OBSTACLES TO ACHIEVEMENT

*Blessed Are Those Who Expect Nothing...For They Shall Not Be Disappointed...*

Anonymous

While it is important for some teachers to change their attitudes and behaviors with regard to teaching and motivating diverse students, it is also especially important that schools and local/state educational agencies abate some of the institutional barriers to school success for Black and Hispanic students. Individual teachers have a unique role to play, as do policy makers and administrators, in eradicating institutional racism and its harmful effects. The existence of institutional racism in our society and our schools cannot be ignored. It can be subtle, but it is pervasive. The very existence of institutional racism can encourage teacher behavior and organizational norms which serve only to reinforce low motivation, underachievement, and poor school and life success in so many Black and Hispanic youth.

The difference between individual and institutional racism is not a difference in intent or visibility. Institutions are fairly stable social arrangements with practices through which collective actions are taken. Individuals often respond to those social arrangements and institutionalized behavioral norms.

Often difficult to recognize, institutional racism is covert, indirect, and sometimes unconscious. The origins of institutional racism are in our most established and respected institutional norms and societal values. All of us frequently act in ways that are socially acceptable. Yet, much of our "socially acceptable" behavior actually reflects long-standing discriminatory assumptions and practices. When these practices become embedded in school systems, schools are likely to act to perpetuate the class differences and racial discrimination that are prevalent in society at large.[1]

The Council on Interracial Books for Children, Inc., in its "Fact Sheet on Institutional Racism," declared that institutional racism exists in economic, government, housing institutions, in the health industry, in the media and in *educational institutions*.[2] (Emphasis added). When some students are denied access to opportunities which others have for rising in the class system, they are victims of institutional racism. The existence of institutional racism in our schools creates situations in which many Black and Hispanic students are enrolled in less challenging educational programs—programs that are less likely to lead to the development of higher order cognitive skills and abilities. Moreover, the existence of institutional racism creates an atmosphere in which some Black and Hispanic students often receive the message that they cannot succeed.[3]

Studies in *The Journal of Negro Education* found that both Black and White teachers perceived that schools and schooling valued neatness, conformity, particular concepts of beauty or appearance, attitudes, language, and behavior. Both White and Black teachers viewed Black males as most negatively "different" from the valued characteristics and White females as the most positive.[4]

Howard found in an analysis of the impact of institutional racism on Black youth a subtle, often subconscious cycle of self-doubt and, in some instances, an avoidance of intellectual competition. Howard concluded that Black youth respond negatively even to rumors of inferiority.[5] These rumors, myths, and innuendoes have a strong subliminal effect on the aspirations and academic achievement of many Black and Hispanic youth. Thus, by early adolescence, many of these students are convinced that academic achievement will not improve their status or benefits. These students learn to adapt to this perceived definition of reality by giving less time and energy to schoolwork. It should not be surprising, therefore, that the longer Black youth stay in school, the farther they fall behind the academic achievements of their White counterparts.[6]

Graves observed that institutional racism brands Black children as inferior from birth.[7] Knowles and Prewitt found that within our educational apparatus, Black students suffer from institutional discrimination in many ways, but particularly in I.Q. testing, classroom ability grouping, and negative teacher attitudes.[8] As Banks and Grambs concluded, the end result of institutional racism is a steady decline in the academic performance of most Black youth.[9]

There have been some efforts to address the prevalence of institutional racism in our schools. In the 1978 decision by U.S. District Court Judge Sarah T. Hughes in the precedent-setting case of *Hawkins v. Dallas Independent School District,* the Dallas public schools were ordered to "eradicate all vestiges of institutional racism from the school system." The court called for extensive training of teachers and counselors along with "institutional and structural changes" in the Dallas public schools. Specifically, the judge concluded that institutional racism can be reduced through efforts to increase teacher expectations and by providing tests and textbooks that accurately represent all ethnic and multicultural groups.

This chapter will discuss some of these school-related obstacles to the achievement of Black and Hispanic students and will offer some suggestions for eliminating these obstacles. In particular, this chapter will focus on:

- the lack of pluralistic curricula.

- the use of instructional strategies and teaching styles that are incompatible with student learning styles.

- academic tracking and ability grouping.
- test bias.

## Lack of Pluralistic Curricula

The call for a holistic and comprehensive change in curricula is not new. In calling for a "total reconceptualization of our views of American history and culture and of the ways they are taught and learned," Gay stressed that cultural pluralism must become an accepted canon of American education.[10]

In a 1977 study by the National Endowment of the Humanities, deficiencies in the knowledge of history and literature were found to be most pronounced among Black and Hispanic youth. Schools were found to be fostering "class bias and elitism" by failing to offer adequate instruction in history and literature to those youth most at risk.[11] This study concluded that when youth were denied *their history, they were unlikely to realize their full potential.* As Cicero wrote, "to know nothing of what happened before you were born is to remain forever a child."[12]

The need for a more pluralistic curriculum has spawned the implementation of the African-Centered (or Afro-centric) curriculum in some urban school districts. The intent of the African-Centered curriculum is to enhance the dignity, pride, self-respect, and motivation of Black youth by enhancing their understanding of their heritage and cultural differences. The following are real examples of rules, and behavioral and procedural norms, which tend to perpetuate institutional racism—even when a multicultural or African centered curriculum exists.

- school policy which indicates that all school cheerleaders should have shoulder-length hair—obviously, this excludes many Black girls.
- school policy which disciplines girls for wearing "colored" stockings, big earrings, or corn row hairstyles—this is likely to cause unfair treatment for Black and Hispanic girls.

- school policy which suspends Black youth for "playing the dozens" when White youth are not disciplined for culturally comparable forms of playful teasing.

- curriculum content which does not emphasize positive aspects of Black and Hispanic life experiences, life styles, or social and behavioral norms.

Whether a school system chooses an African-Centered curriculum or a curricular model rooted in multiculturalism, it must do more than teach history. The school program must also reflect changes in attitudes, teaching strategies, assessment procedures, value orientation, and the substance of what is taught. It is important to seek pluralism in the curriculum through efforts to determine

- what is being taught.

- why it is being taught.

- who is providing the instruction.

- how the instruction is being provided.

***What is being taught is important.*** All too often the school curriculum focuses on information that is totally irrelevant to the status or survival of Black and Hispanic youth. The curriculum must be revised to foster an appreciation of all of the positive components of the students' racial or cultural group as well as the most accurate portrayal of history from the perspective of that particular racial or cultural group.

***Education for what?*** When forced to answer this question, educators must make certain they are not just imparting the skills and knowledge needed by students to just "make do" in society. Black and Hispanic students must be convinced that they are being groomed and prepared for careers that will bring them professional gratification and financial security. It is important, therefore, that education make certain that students are not put in vocational/technical or low-level tracks that only prepare them for menial labor or dead-end jobs.

*Who is educating Black and Hispanic students?*
Fewer numbers of Blacks and Hispanics are seeking to become
teachers. More effort must be put into the recruitment of
Black and Hispanic teachers, and *male* teachers in particular.
The pool of Black and Hispanic male teachers is expected to
dwindle to below 5% by the year 2000. Black and Hispanic
youth are likely to be more responsive to teachers of their race
and culture. However, White teachers who are capable of em-
bracing multiple teaching strategies, pluralistic classroom environments, and multicultural course materials can have a
positive impact on the achievement of their Black and Hispanic students.

*How the instruction is provided is central to under-
standing who internalizes the knowledge imparted.* Instructional strategies and teaching styles must tap the full
range of student potential. This is discussed in more detail in
the following section.

## Making Teaching and Learning Styles More Congruent

Students who find their culture and learning styles reflected in both the substance and the organization of the instructional program are more likely to be motivated and less
likely to be disruptive. They're more likely to benefit from
their learning experience. In her book, *Black Children: Their
Roots, Culture and Learning Styles*, Janice Hale-Benson suggests that formal education has not worked for many Black
youth because it has not employed the teaching styles that
correspond with students' learning styles. Benson observes
that Black youth have barely mastered the norms of their own
culture when they are confronted with teaching styles that are
incompatible with their accepted learning patterns.[13]

When this incongruity between teaching and learning
styles exists, Black children become less motivated and more
likely to question their self-worth. When Black youth find
learning difficult, many often blame themselves and develop

animosity toward the educational environment. Many Hispanic students react similarly.

Before teachers can understand and appreciate the learning styles preferred by students, it is important to understand the role that culture plays in shaping learning styles. Culture shapes cognitive development, children's approach to academic tasks, and their behavior in traditional academic settings.[14] Cultural conflict can occur when children have not had experiences that provide them with the kind of information that is used and valued in school.

To reach all children, educators must expand their repertoire of instructional strategies to encompass the various approaches children use to learn. In writing about Black children's learning styles, Hale-Benson suggests that many Black youth employ people-oriented, relational, and field dependent/sensitive approaches to learning rather than the analytical style favored in most school structures. The obvious must be stressed, however. All Black and Hispanic children do *not* use the same learning style.

People-oriented learning is a learning style derived from African heritage. Because many Black youth learn in their pre-school years through extensive social interaction, some Black youth may have more difficulty than White students in settings where learning takes place primarily through the use of educational hardware, technology, books, listening stations, learning centers, television, programmed instruction, learning kits, and other objects.[15] Because of the differences in culture, some Black youth can benefit from intensive personal interaction with teachers who provide rapport, nonverbal support, and affection.

Research also indicates that a high percentage of Black and Hispanic children are "field-dependent." The field-dependent or field-sensitive learner tends to be aware of the social and personal relevance of the learning experience. It matters to these youngsters that the materials and concepts are related to their own experience and are neither abstract nor isolated.[16] Field-dependent learners prefer student-centered, more personal environments. The field-dependent learner prefers small-group activities and thrives when allowed opportunities to exchange information with peers. Field-independent learners, on the other hand, are more interested in concepts for their own sake. These students function very successfully in self-structured learning; enjoy learning isolated information; and like to work in independent, teacher-centered, impersonal environments.

Children who are field-dependent prefer to work together for the benefit of the group in an atmosphere where the pace of learning is set by the momentum of the group rather than by imposed time constraints. These youth find it difficult to function in field-independent environments, where achievement results from individual and often competitive efforts.

Some major differences between field-dependent and field-independent learners are presented in Table II.

## TABLE II

### LEARNING PREFERENCES

| Field Independent Students | Field Dependent Students |
| --- | --- |
| Independent projects, working alone | Group projects, sharing, discussions |
| Hypothesis-testing approaches | Personal examples, anecdotes, stories |
| Solving problems | Relating learning to own experiences |
| A focus on details, moving from specific to general (phonics, structured rules in spelling and mathematics) | A focus on the big picture, an overview moving from the general to the specific (whole-word, language experience, reasons for rules) |
| Clear grading criteria with specific feedback | Praise, assurance, working to please others, frequent interaction with teachers |
| Teacher-centered environment | Student-centered environment |

(Adapted from Howard, Bessie C. *Learning to Persist/Persisting to Learn.* *Mid-Atlantic Center for Race Equity, The American University: Washington, D.C., 1987)*

Reprinted from Kuykendall, Crystal *Improving Black Student Achievement by Enhancing Student Self-Image*, Mid-Atlantic Center for Race Equity, The American University, Washington, D.C. 1989.

Given what we know about the impact of learning styles on student performance, educators who are serious about enhancing the achievement and motivation of Black and Hispanic youth must be willing to use a variety of activities to stimulate interest and facilitate student growth. Research on learning styles indicates that, for these students, active learning is more effective than passive drill and practice exercises. Similarly, Black and Hispanic youth are likely to respond favorably to think-pair-share activities, lively group discussions, cooperative learning, group projects, and telling of stories about personal experiences.

Teachers will also discover that many "active learners" also are encouraged when course content and classroom activities relate to something in their own life experiences. Of real significance, however, is the powerful impact of a teacher's genuine and sincere interest in the well-being of the student. Personal compliments, praise, enthusiasm, and even hugs often work wonders in keeping Black and Hispanic youth interested and excited about learning.

Good summarized how teachers communicate expectations through the following behaviors toward perceived underachievers.[17]

- providing students with general, often insincere praise.

- providing them with less feedback.

- demanding less effort of them.

- interrupting them more often

- seating them farther away from the teacher.

- paying less attention to them.

- calling on them less often.

- waiting less time for them to respond to questions.

- criticizing them more often.

- smiling at them less.

Most assuredly, teachers can reverse the consequences of low expectations by avoiding these behaviors. Murnane also found that youth will feel more positive about their abilities and self-worth when teachers provide sincere and requisite support and encouragement.[18]

## Academic Tracking and Ability Grouping

Considered one of the more blatant forms of institutional racism, tracking is one means of denying youth equal educational opportunities (*Hobson v. Hansen*, 1971). Therefore, it has been outlawed in some jurisdictions. The failure rate of many Black and Hispanic youth can be attributed in part to "between and within" classroom ability grouping, which fosters development of a "caste system" in school that allows for downward, but not upward, mobility.[19]

Lawler found that when children are tracked they are deprived of the opportunity to develop the skills needed for success in the labor force. Moreover, Lawler found that Black youth respond to tracking by being truant or by withdrawing mentally and emotionally from the learning experience.[20]

The June 1989 report by the Carnegie Council on Adolescent Development, *Turning Points*, found that 25 percent of 10- to 17-year-olds in the United States are extremely vulnerable to school failure. The report recommended changes in the middle school grades which included smaller, more family-like school environments and an *end to tracking students by ability* (emphasis is added). The report states:[21]

> In theory, this between-class "tracking" reduces the heterogeneity of the classes and enables teachers to adjust instruction to students' knowledge and skills. Greater achievement is then possible for both "low-" and "high-ability" students.

In practice, this kind of tracking has proven to be one of the most divisive and damaging school practices in existence. Time and again, young people placed in lower academic tracks or classes, often during the middle grades, are locked into dull, repetitive instructional programs leading at best to minimum competencies.

Tracking and ability grouping are likely to send subliminal messages to Black and Hispanic youth that White and middle class students are going to have opportunities for a greater range of knowledge and, therefore, opportunities for more lifelong success.

The extensive tracking of Black and Hispanic students in disproportionate numbers was outlined in a 1980 study that showed that 24.1 percent of the public school population was Black and Hispanic but only 13.8 percent of those students were in gifted-and-talented programs. The over-representation of Blacks and Hispanics in lower-ability groups, as well as in vocational and general tracks, also was documented by Harrischefeger and Wiley.[22]

If educators are to enhance the achievement of Black and Hispanic students, they must eradicate tracking, ability grouping and the negative messages conveyed through these strategies. Oakes saw tracking as a major contributor to "mediocre schooling" and described the following consequences:[23]

- initial differences among students are exaggerated rather than accommodated.

- school officials accept the achievement of a few at the expense of the majority.

- most students have mediocre classroom experiences due to curricular and instructional inequalities.

- barriers develop to prevent success for Blacks and Hispanics.

Instead of tracking and ability grouping, teachers should make effective use of heterogeneous grouping and cooperative learning strategies. This does *not* mean that students will merely sit side-by-side at the same table and talk to each other as they do individual assignments. Nor does this approach mean that a group of students will put their names on an assignment that only one student will complete. There are five basic elements of heterogeneous grouping/cooperative learning:[24]

- *mixed achievement/accomplishments.* Students with differing levels of academic accomplishment work together. Usually, high, middle, and underachieving students are put in cooperative learning groups.

- *positive interdependence.* Each member of the group understands that there will be mutual goals (goal interdependence); divisions of labor (task interdependence); dividing of materials, resources, or information among group members (resource interdependence); assigning of students to differing roles (role interdependence) based on non-academic or academic strengths; and joint rewards (reward interdependence).

- *face-to-face interaction.* It is the interaction between students, verbal interchange, and mutual support that affect education outcomes.

- *individual accountability.* The achievement of each student is to be maximized. Students must provide appropriate support and assistance to one another.

- *use of interpersonal and small group skills.* Teachers do not want to place socially unskilled students in small groups without first teaching the social skills needed for collaboration. Students must be motivated to use their real social skills. Students also must be given the time and procedures for analyzing how well their learning groups are functioning and the extent to which students are employing their social skills to help all group members to achieve and to maintain effective working relations within the group.

If done correctly, the use of heterogeneous grouping and cooperative learning has the advantage of being more democratic. The content, teaching methods, classroom climate, and teacher-student interaction of heterogeneous classrooms often resemble average and upper track classes.[25] Studies have found that this provision of a common learning experience to students with different backgrounds, interests, cultures, and plans for the future—in small groups—results in high achievement for students at all previous "tracking" levels.[26]

## Test Bias

Culturally biased tests should not be used for the placement of Black and Hispanic youth because they do not reflect the true ability of many students. Many tests, such as the Stanford-Binet Intelligence Test, include items that assess moral opinions and other values that reflect social class bias rather than ability.[27] For example, Taylor found that many standard tests reflect communication-related biases such as those presented in Table III. I.Q. tests are considered by many experts as one tool used to deny equal educational opportunities to Black and Hispanic youth. In his study of the impact of I.Q. testing on student placement, Asa Hilliard suggested that educators must find alternatives to I.Q. testing in order to identify giftedness in Black and Hispanic children.[28] In California, Indiana, and some other states, the courts have addressed the issue and concluded that "minorities" should not be placed through the use of biased I.Q. testing and other instruments.

The consequences of inappropriate tests include:

- the over-representation of Blacks and Hispanics in special education classes and low-ability groups and tracks.

- the alienation and physical or psychological withdrawal of underachieving students from the learning process due to their inability to master mainstream culture well enough to do well on culturally biased exams.

- negative attitudes toward the schools on the part of parents who have come to recognize and appreciate the social skills of their children and who, themselves, felt victimized by culturally biased tests when they were in school.

- lower expectations of teachers who fail to understand that lower scores of some Black and Hispanic youth on tests is more an indication of cultural conflict than low intelligence.

Lawler felt that it was nearly impossible to develop a culture-free test, because no test can incorporate materials and skills that are common to all cultures.[29] However, while teachers must still use standardized tests, they can develop other instruments that can enhance student confidence and academic self-image. The use of criterion-referenced tests that are based on what has actually been taught in school can allow students to show mastery of specific materials. These tests are unlikely to use structural formats (e.g., multiple choice and timed segments).

### TABLE III

### SOURCES OF COMMUNICATION AND COMMUNICATION RELATED BIASES IN TESTS AND ASSESSMENT PROCEDURES

| | |
|---|---|
| Situational Bias | Mismatches between Examiner and Examinee Regarding the Social Rules of Language, e.g., Sarcastic answer to obvious question<br>Examiner: What time does the clock say?<br>Examinee: Everybody knows clocks don't talk. |
| Directions Bias | Test Directions Involve Linguistic Complexities Unfamiliar to the Examinee, e.g., "None of the following are true except..." incorrectly interpreted as "All of the following are true except..." |

**TABLE III (continued)**

| | |
|---|---|
| Value Bias | Examinee is Required to Exhibit a Particular Moral or Ethical Preference, e.g., One who is dishonest is<br>a) an offender<br>b) a politician<br>c) an ambassador<br>d) an officer |
| Linguistic Bias | Test Presumes that Examinee is Competent in Standard English, e.g., Which sentence is ungrammatical:<br>a) They saw Rose<br>b) You done it wrong<br>c) My brother has never eaten<br>d) Don't use too much |
| Format Bias | Test Procedures or Requirements are Inconsistent with Examinee's Cognitive and/or Learning Style, e.g., Select the *best* answer to the following |
| Cultural Bias | Examiner Erroneously Interprets Cultural Practices of Examinee, e.g., Child who exhibits silence as a natural reaction to an unfamiliar adult examiner is diagnosed as non-verbal, or who does not respond quickly to test items as unknowledgeable |

From Taylor, Orlando: *Cross-Cultural Communication: An Essential Dimension of Effective Education. Mid-Atlantic Center for Race Equity.* The American University, Washington, D.C. 1987.

Teachers also can evaluate students with assessment instruments more likely to measure true ability. These include oral exams (especially when a child has shown difficulty in taking written tests), class projects, group assignments, and other simulated materials designed to provide more accurate indices of understanding and skill mastery.

# Notes

1. Knowles, L. and Prewitt, K. *Institutional Racism in America*. Englewood Cliffs, New Jersey: Prentice-Hall, 1969.

2. *Council on Interracial Books for Children*. Inc. Op. Cit.

3. Hammond, L. *Equality and Excellence: Educational Status of Black Americans*. New York: The College Board, 1985.

4. Washington, V. "Racial Differences in Teacher Perceptions of First and Fourth Grade Pupils on Selected Characteristics." *Journal of Negro Education*; Vol. 51 No. 1, Winter 1982.

5. Howard, J. "Race and How It Affects Our Every Day Life" *Detroit Free Press*, December 12, 1985.

6. Berube, M. *Education and Poverty: Effective Schooling in the U.S.* Westport, Connecticut: Greenwood Press, 1984.

7. Graves, E. "Public Education: Broken Promise for Many." *Black Enterprise*, September, 1978.

8. Knowles, L. and Prewitt, K. Op. Cit.

9. Banks, J. and Grambs, J., eds. *Black Self Concept*. New York, N.Y.: McGraw-Hill Book Co., 1972.

10. Gay, G. "Achieving Educational Equality Through Curriculum Desegregation" *Phi Delta Kappen*, 1990.

11. Cheyney, L., Fine M. Ravitch, D. *American Memory: A Report on the Humanities in the Nation's Public Schools*. National Endowment for the Humanities, 1987.

12. Ibid.

13. Hale-Benson, J. *Black Children: Their Roots, Culture and Learning Styles*. Provo, UT: Brigham Young University Press, 1982.

14. Ibid.

15. Ibid.

16. Hale-Bensen, J. Op. Cit.

17. Good, T.L. "Teacher Expectations an Student Perceptions: A Decade of Research." *Educational Leadership*, February 1981.

18. Murnane, R. "Empirical Analysis of the Relations Between School Resource and the Cognitive Development of Black Inner City Children In a Large Urban School System (New Haven)." Taken from *Final Report on Schooling of Young Children: Cognitive and Affective Outcomes*, National Institute of Education, 1975.

19. Rist, R. "Study of How Teachers Treat Children Differently." In *Final Report on the Schooling of Young Children: Cognitive and Affective Outcomes*, National Institute of Education, 1978.

20. Lawler, J.M. *I.Q. Heredity and Racism*. New York, N.Y.: International Publishers, 1978.

21. Carnegie Council on Adolescent Development "Turning Points: Education in America in the 21st Century" Washington, D.C., 1989 Taken from Kuykendall, C. *Improving Black Student Achievement By Enhancing Student Self-Image*, Washington, D.C.: Mid-Atlantic Center for Race, Equity of American University, 1989.

22. Harrischefeger, A. and Wiley, P.E. "A Merit Assessment of Vocational Education Programs in Secondary Schools." A statement to the Subcommittee on Elementary, Secondary and Vocational Education, September, 1980.

23. Oakes, J. "Keeping Track: The Policy and Practice of Curriculum Inequality" *Phi Delta Kappan*, September, 1986 Taken from Kuykendall, Crystal, Op. Cit.

24. Hale, Op. Cit.

25. Hale, Op. Cit.

26. Parker, W. "I Ain't No Group, I'm Me." In *Strategies For Educational Change*, McMillan Press, 1981.

27. Hilliard, A. "Alternatives to I.Q. Testing: An Approach to the Identification of Gifted Minority Children" Final Report to the California State Department of Education, 1976.

28. Ibid.

28. Lawler, J. M. I.Q. *Heredity and Racism*. New York, N.Y.: International Publishers, 1978.

# 4 MOTIVATING THE "UN-MOTIVATED"

*All children want to learn and can learn...*

Marva Collins, 1990
*Marva Collins' Way*

Much has been said about the lack of "motivation" of Black, Hispanic, and poor students. Many of these students fail to reach their full potential not because they don't want to learn, but because they are put in situations in which it becomes nearly impossible to learn. The previous chapters have provided insight and information which can, hopefully, facilitate attitudinal, behavioral, and structural changes in our schools. This chapter goes a step further. It is unfortunate, but many youths who exhibit low motivation are simply responding to the behavior of some of their unmotivated teachers. This chapter should excite teachers about the roles they can play in motivating so many children.

I do not want to suggest that most teachers lack the desire to teach—quite the contrary. As I have said before, most teachers are especially well-intentioned and sincere. Many well-meaning and well-intentioned teachers are actually frustrated, however, by a perceived inability to reach Black and Hispanic youth. It is this frustration that I would like to address and change. Black and Hispanic youth will respond positively to a learning environment which is conducive to school success. When teachers allow the restraints of low expectations, inappropriate curriculum, incongruent teaching styles, ability grouping, and test bias to determine what they do and how they "motivate" students, they can be sure of at least one thing—neither teacher nor student will be successful.

Black and Hispanic students must believe, first of all, that academic achievement will improve their status, benefits, and general prosperity. As noted previously, they must have "hope" for better lives. Many unmotivated teachers never really provide that hope because they don't foster a belief in these students that they *can* succeed academically. As a result, many Black and Hispanic youth see themselves as trapped in a society with limited or nonexistent opportunities for significant and legitimate upward mobility. The current existence of a growing "underclass" of Black and Hispanic youth is an indication that many of these youth see an absence of opportunity for significant change in income, social roles, and social class status. Consequently, they stop seeking academic success or "real" work in mainstream society after leaving school and opt instead for survival through more traditional deviant systems—robbery, burglary, drug sale, larceny, and murder.[1]

There are many things educators can do to rekindle the excitement of Black and Hispanic students. I say "rekindle" because I have yet to hear of a kindergartener who was not excited about starting school. Black and Hispanic youth are just like all other children who want so much to please—*and* to learn. Educators must be willing to learn and grow with their students.

The following tips are provided to help teachers "rekindle" student motivation and academic success and, in the process, derive greater gratification from the teaching profession:

## Ten Tips for Teaching Terrific Children

1.  Develop "strong bonds" with diverse students.

2.  Identify and build on the strengths of all students.

3.  Help students overcome fear of failure.

4.  Help students overcome rejection of success.

5. Set short- and long-term goals with and for your students.

6. Develop teaching styles that are more congruent with the learning style preferences of Black and Hispanic students.

7. Use homework and television to *your* advantage.

8. Communicate so that your real intentions are understood.

9. Establish a climate where children receive the ongoing support and encouragement they need to succeed.

10. Strengthen relations between the home and school.

A brief discussion of each of these tips follows:

## 1. Develop Strong Bonds with Diverse Students

Any teacher who *really* loves children can motivate children. However, that love must be unconditional. In too many instances, a teacher's love and appreciation of a student is "condition subsequent," that is, the result of certain behavior and abilities in students. Instead, the teacher's love and appreciation should be "condition precedent." Her love would encourage favorable behavior and enhance abilities in students. When a student detects teacher detachment, disinterest, or disrespect, social and personal "bonds" are weakened.

In their research on the causes of delinquency. Fagan and Jones determined that it is the weakening of personal and social bonds with adults that leads to negative peer influences. Schools must provide strong external bonds through efforts to improve achievement, efforts to involve youth in activities perceived as important, and efforts to enhance students' belief in their own abilities and self-determination.[2]

Educators can build student relationships characterized by mutual trust. However, in order to do this, teachers must show a respect for the student and his or her culture, life experiences, and unique learning style. Teachers must see themselves as "learners" as well as teachers. Through a spirit of mutual inquiry, teachers can build bonds with students that foster support and augment achievement motivation.

Once mutual trust is established, the teacher can involve the student in a learning process that takes into account the needs of both student and teacher, as well as the needs of the school (or system) and the needs of society in general. Even when it appears that these needs are in conflict, they are not necessarily at odds.

For example, the student may speak in a non-standard English dialect. The student may be unaware of the *need* for him to be able to speak standard English. The teacher, however—and the school—share a need for that child to be able to speak standard English. Society has a commensurate need for leaders and laborers who are skilled in standard forms of communication. The teacher can help children understand that standard English is required for them to achieve legitimate economic success in this country. At the same time, the teacher should show that the child's previously learned language skills also are valued and have a place in society. In casual conversation students may choose to speak in a dialect, be it Spanish or "Black English." Both are legitimate forms of expression.

The needs of the teacher, the school, the student, and society can all be met through instruction which respects student differences in dialect and culture. An excited, understanding, and caring teacher can bond with a student, regardless of background, language, race, or culture. Further, teachers can show their acceptance of students' speech through the use of poems, stories, and plays that contain dialect. Teachers may occasionally build rhythmic speech patterns and activities into lesson plans and accept slang or cultural dialect while stressing the appropriate and inappropriate uses of such language.

## 2. Identify and Build on the Strengths of All Students

In many of our schools, too much emphasis is placed on identifying student deficiencies. Once deficiencies are discerned, many educators spend an inordinate amount of time reminding both the student and the parent that those deficiencies exist. If students are allowed to believe that significant adults in their lives, i.e., teachers and parents, see them as incompetent and inferior, many students are likely to see themselves in much the same manner. Their destiny in life often is determined by how they see themselves in their formative years.

All children have non-academic gifts and talents. Every teacher should put two adjectives that describe two of the child's non-academic strengths next to that child's name in the roll book. During the course of the instructional program, children should be provided with opportunities to display their non-academic strengths and talents in ways that enhance academic learning. For example, students can use dramatic or musical skills in role playing or debating.[3]

In teaching parts of speech to Black and Hispanic students in Newark public schools, I discovered quickly the strengths of my dramatic and assertive students. I had my more "dramatic" students perform skits where each person was given a specific role to play. Someone was a noun and someone else was an adjective who had to find the noun he was to describe. Similarly the "adverb" was told to stand next to the noun, rather than the verb; "commas" were told to put themselves in the wrong sequence; "participles" were told to "dangle." The rest of the class had fun specifying where each "part" (person) was supposed to be. My students learned parts of speech through my efforts to teach to *their* strengths.

When a teacher builds on student strengths, it's easier to help that student to clarify his own aspirations for improved behavior and to diagnose the gaps between his aspirations and his present level of performance. The teacher then presents him/herself as a person who appreciates the real worth, feelings, and ideas of that student. The word "teacher" has its roots in the Latin word meaning "to lead or to draw out." Good teachers can bring out the best in every student by acknowledging and strengthening individual and cultural strengths rather than causing self-doubt through a preoccupation with the student's weaknesses.

Family and cultural strengths can be acknowledged through class discussions or writing activities that allow students to relate family and personal experiences that have facilitated their growth, evoked special feelings, or taught them a sense of responsibility. Teachers also can use activities that emphasize those things that make the heritage of a particular student so special, or allow students to engage in dramatic readings or role plays where they have opportunities to dramatize some of the cultural values and behaviors of all races.

In building on the strengths students bring to school, teachers can bring out their hidden potential, thereby strengthening both their social and academic self-images. By building confidence, teachers will be able to abate the fear of failure that causes many Black and Hispanic students to "give up" before their full potential has been realized.

### 3. Helping Students to Overcome Fear of Failure

All of us have, at some point in our lives, refrained from doing something because we felt we would not succeed. Fear of failure is real. If a child has experienced failure before, he or she does not want to experience it again. A person with a low self-image is likely to use fear of failure as an excuse for giving up or avoiding effort altogether. When individuals have strong self-images, fear of failure can be motivational.

Teachers can help students to overcome fear of failure by first letting every child know that he or she *will* succeed in the learning environment. Teachers must encourage students to see all failure as a learning experience. The feeling of confidence that comes from encouragement will make it easier for failing students to use failure constructively and to persist. Persistence is a learned behavior.[4] Teachers will be hard pressed to teach persistence unless they have it themselves. This means teachers cannot give up on children and must let children know that their support and faith will not evaporate.

Many children who fear academic failure have already overcome fear of failure in social and recreational activities. Teachers can remind children of the experience they had in learning to ride a bike, for example. Although *every* bike rider fell down, children who learned to ride bikes can appreciate the fact that they were able to learn to ride because they *refused* to give up. Similarly, each child can ride the bike called "reading," the bike called "math," the bike called "higher-order thinking," the bike called "science"—but only if he or she *refuses* to give up.

A teacher can help overcome fear of failure in students by informing students of the teacher's intent to involve them in the development of mutually acceptable criteria and methods for measuring progress. By showing students the intention to meet them "where they are," teachers can encourage students to strive for the "3 Ds"—*Determination, Diligence,* and *Discipline.*

Finally, confidence can be enhanced and fear of failure overcome when teachers use activities that build on the non-academic strengths of students and take time to nurture and extol these strengths in the classroom.[5] Students must know that they have opportunities for "legitimate" success through the effective use and channeling of their non-academic strengths. Once they realize they can shoot for specific careers and professional goals that are based on their strengths, children are more likely to be motivated to overcome their academic deficiencies. Table IV presents a listing of some non-academic strengths many Black and Hispanic students are likely to have, and indicates the possible academic or career outlets that can be encouraged as a result of those strengths.

## TABLE IV

### MATCHING NON-ACADEMIC STRENGTHS WITH CAREER CHOICES

| Non-academic strengths or qualities | Possible academic or career outlet |
|---|---|
| moral responsibility | social service, teaching |
| compassion | psychology, medicine, nursing |
| diplomacy | politics |
| humor and wit | law, writing |
| sensitivity | counseling, teaching |
| independence | business, science |
| courage | civic activism, advocacy organization |
| altruism | social work, nursing, community organizing, environmental work |
| manual dexterity | computers, carpentry, graphic arts, locksmith |
| talent for innovation and improvisation | law, media, engineering, architecture, politics |
| mechanical achievement | mechanics, plumbing, electrical work, drafting |
| expressive achievement | performing arts, writing, interior design |
| culinary achievement | chef, caterer, dietitian |
| physical prowess | fire fighter, emergency medical technician |
| social achievement | hotel management, sales |

## 4. Helping Students to Overcome a Rejection of Success

Some Black and Hispanic youth reject "success" as a "White" behavioral norm or as a norm pleasing to the teacher, who in many instances is perceived as "the enemy." These children are then unlikely to put forth very much effort.[6] Teachers can help students overcome this rejection of success by helping them to become more goal oriented.

Success is the progressive realization of a worthwhile goal. Children who reject success generally have not established either short- or long-range goals. Many Black and Hispanic youth fail to set goals because they feel they have minimal control over their fate and will be unable to make a difference in the outcome of a problem, project, experiment, or grade.[7] This belief, common to lower-income students, has been labeled an "external locus of control." Many lower-income youth, as a result of school biases, see no relationship between hard work and success. Additionally, some Black and Hispanic students may have been taught by their parents that rewards very often can be discriminately and inconsistently dispensed.[8] Some Black and Hispanic youth may even fail to set goals because they have little knowledge of what are acceptable goals.

The earlier a child learns the importance of setting goals, the earlier that child will learn the discipline and the necessity for delayed gratification if one is to realize challenging goals. Teachers must understand that Black and Hispanic students, especially, need to believe that goals are attainable and that effort will be rewarded. Educators can instill confidence in students by allowing them to set short-range goals for which they *do* receive support, recognition, and quick reward.

I have already discussed the powerful impact of peer pressure and the "us versus them mentality" likely to develop in some Black and Hispanic students. In a study of low-income Black students at a Washington, D.C., school, peer pressure, and the fear of being accused of abandoning one's social identity, were cited as major reasons why many Black students refused to study, shunned standard English, and avoided what they perceived to be "White" interests (the symphony, opera, and the humanities).[9]

Some students were ambivalent toward academic success because they defined it as a "White perogative" and didn't want to typify White behavior. Spending long hours in study was considered by these youth as emulating Whites. Other students indicated pressure from peers not to excel for fear of being "labelled" homosexual. Many educational institutions have actually contributed to the belief held by some Black and Hispanic students that academic success is "for Whites only" through tracking, ability grouping, and programs which appear to students as discriminatory. Many Black and Hispanic students are made to feel they must "act White" to be successful.

Teachers must help students to understand and appreciate the fact that success is *very definitely* part of the Black and Hispanic experience. Rather than foster the belief that academic achievement is a "White" prerogative, teachers must help Black and Hispanic students to understand and appreciate the standards for excellence set by diverse races and cultures around the world.

If teachers are going to abate the notion among these students that they cannot be successful, that they must choose between their culture and that of the school, teachers also must take steps to eliminate the effects of institutional racism. Black and Hispanic youth are more likely to see academic achievement as a "White" prerogative when there is an over-representation of Blacks and Hispanics in special education classes or lower ability groups. Teachers and administrators must not only eliminate policies and programs that foster such over-representation, they should also:

- Review school policy and revise or eliminate rules that punish students for cultural habits, e.g., wearing African or corn-row hairstyles, signifying or playing the dozens, or being loud or expressive.

- Review instructional materials that belittle, exclude, or stereotype races and cultures. Add materials that are multicultural in all subject areas at all grade levels. If certain biased materials are kept, teachers must know how to use these materials in non-biased ways.

- Develop a basic familiarity with Black and Hispanic culture through staff-development sessions or personal efforts to enhance knowledge. Such efforts might include more reading, visits to art shows or museums, and participating in social events for Black and Hispanic groups.

- Eliminate the word "minorities" from the vocabulary. Schools are preparing students for a *universe* where people of color are not in the "minority" at all.

- Use flexible, heterogeneous, and cooperative groupings rather than ability groupings and tracking.

- Ensure that schools in predominantly Black and Hispanic neighborhoods are financed at least at the same level as schools in predominantly White neighborhoods.

- Incorporate the provision of equal opportunity in the classroom as part of the teacher evaluation process.

Most importantly, teachers must help Black and Hispanic students understand that school success will not require a rejection of their home or family culture.

## 5. Setting Short- and Long-Term Goals

Black and Hispanic students must be convinced that they can be what they *choose* to be in life. Teachers must help them understand that if they can "conceive it in their hearts and believe it, they can achieve it." As noted previously, these students also must be taught the importance of persistence.

In Table V, there is a "Success Chart" that can be used to help students set short- or long-range goals. This chart should be completed in the presence of the teacher. Students should first identify a goal they want to achieve by the age of 25. Next, students, with the help of the teacher, should list their outstanding qualities and those things that are likely to help them reach their goals. They also should develop specific strategies for achieving this long-term goal. Teachers can help by acknowledging student strengths and by letting the students know their intent is to help them reach their goal. Teachers also can indicate a willingness to help students overcome those weaknesses the students feel might be impeding their progress.

### TABLE V
### THE SUCCESS CHART

Student Name _____

**Goal** (Something you would like to have, become, or accomplish by the age of 25):

_____

_____

_____

_____

**HELP:**

List qualities or characteristics you possess that will help you reach *your goal:*

_____

_____

_____

**HINDER:**

List things that could possibly hurt or limit your efforts to reach *your goal:*

_____

_____

_____

**Strategies for achieving this goal:**

1. _____

2. _____

3. _____

NOTE: This same procedure can be used for short-range goals (e.g., Something you'd like to do within the next three weeks). For short-range goals, list specific steps to be taken and include a time frame.

Taken from Kuykendall, C. *Improving Black Student Achievement by Enhancing Student Self-Image*, Mid Atlantic Equity Center of American University, Washington, D.C. 1989.

In addition to the use of this success chart, teachers can:

- Schedule a monthly "show-and-tell" in which students share with the class non-school-related goals they have set and accopmlished.

- Have weekly reviews of famous Black and Hispanic Americans who have achieved their goals. Continue to remind students that success is very much a part of *their* culture and experience.

- Applaud all efforts students put forth to reach their goals.

- Set monthly academic achievement goals with and for each student and share them with parents or guardians.

- Assist students in developing sequential strategies for meeting goals.

- Help students to see failure as a learning experience by discussing failure as part of the road to success.

Students can also be inspired by the role model they see in their teachers, especially their Black and Hispanic teachers. Far too many teachers are discouraged because they believe their students lack adequate role models in their homes and communities. Rather than concern themselves with the influences outside of the school over which they have no control, teachers can make the most of the time they have with students. Remember, most students spend more time interacting with their "school family" (approximately six hours every day) than they spend interacting with their "home family." A teacher's exemplary behavior and aspirations can have a tremendous influence on students' drive and goal orientation. Finally, teachers and administrators must be willing to reward students who fulfill their goals. Students are motivated by rewards; and when success is rewarded, it is reinforced.

For example, Eastern High School in Washington, D.C., sponsors four "Student of the Month" awards. The winners, top students who have been recommended by teachers, get $15, a certificate, their pictures on a plaque in the school lobby, breakfast with a Kiwanis Club member, and lunch on Capitol Hill with the principal and a school board member. This program is designed to boost the image of students who are doing well, and to make success a cultural norm for the school.

Educators must work very hard to dispel the belief that it doesn't pay to do well academically. Children can be motivated to succeed through inspirational examples. As often as possible, teachers should allow students to discuss local success stories, such as:

- the experiences of city or county council representatives who might have lived in the students' neighborhood or attended their school and who set goals they reached.

- the accomplishments of elementary or high school alumni who also reached goals they set.

- the triumphs of local business persons or community leaders or family members who overcame setbacks.

- the experiences of local entertainers or sports heroes.

- the road to success taken by educators, including their own teachers.

- examine the lives of national heroes, past and present, especially those whose early lives were similar to the students'.

Keep students inspired and let them know victory can and will be theirs. They have to believe in their own abilities and the power within themselves in order to reach personal goals.

## 6. Develop Appropriate Teaching Styles

Many Black and Hispanic students respond favorably to extensive interaction with the teacher and other peers. I strongly encourage hugging, encouraging pats on the back, and other gestures that may involve touching in a supportive and nurturing manner, especially for younger children. The contact should be sincere and supportive, not intrusive. Teachers should also supplement the use of objects (i.e., computers and other learning devices) with person-to-person interaction, proximity, and lots of assurance. In addition, teachers should be sure to:

- speak in a comforting, consoling, but firm and determined voice.

- demonstrate fairness in the treatment of students.

- incorporate humor in their interaction with the class or individual students.

- develop rapport with students, and suggest that other test givers do the same, before administering an exam.

Maintain a high level of openness and acceptance with Black youth who engage in "stage setting." These are activities deemed important and necessary by some Black youth before engaging in an assignment (e.g., pencil sharpening, rearranging posture, checking paper and writing space, asking for repeat directions, and even checking perceptions with their neighbors). Many teachers are likely to perceive "stage setting" as an attempt to avoid work or disrupt class. However, this is an important activity for many Black youth.[10] Teachers can convey understanding and an acceptance of this need by allowing a few minutes for "stage setting" activities.

Demonstrate higher academic expectations. Teachers must not just tell students they believe in their abilities, they must *show* them. Convince these students that teachers believe in them and want them to excel by:

- using the classroom walls to display the work of all students in areas where they are skilled.

- writing encouraging notes on students' papers and to parents or guardians of elementary school students.

- maintaining a warm, inviting classroom climate through the use of appropriate attitudes and behaviors and bright and bold colors at all grade levels.

- encouraging students' natural exuberance, toning it down if necessary, without making students feel that they are wrong to show emotion.

- recognizing the knowledge and achievement of Black and Hispanic students in *all* areas.

Scheduling one-on-one sessions with students to discuss their weekly, monthly, and long-range goals is also helpful. Teachers can monitor progress and provide insight for ongoing improvement. If a heavy class load precludes meeting with each student, meet with a significant portion of students who require more attention.

Use a variety of other teaching strategies. Peer tutoring or coaching helps students on both sides. The phrase "each one teach one" should be a part of the class motto. Make good use of the "Buddy Game" which calls for pairing students who will be "buddy" to one another. Students spend time with their "buddies"—getting homework assignments in their absence, learning and sharing skills, information, and strategies. Encourage "buddies" to each make a list of all the strengths and talents that make their buddies special!

Have a "King" or "Queen" for a day where every child gets to play the part of "Class King" or "Class Queen." (Choose by lottery or alphabetically.) The King or Queen's buddy comes before the class and takes a few minutes to share everything *good* about his or her buddy. The teacher also shares good things about the honored student.

## 7) Use Homework and Television to Your Advantage

Homework should promote cooperation and communication among the teacher, the student, and the parent. It should help the child develop responsibility and independence, master a skill, and understand what has been taught. It should also encourage children to learn new things and keep parents informed about what their children are learning in school.[11]

Given the anticipated benefits of homework, teachers can make it a more powerful experience by:

- giving students homework projects that can involve members of their families; i.e., doing a family tree, assessing family strengths and virtues, writing fictional stories which feature family members as heroes/heroines, etc.

- giving students homework assignments which play to *their* strengths. A student athlete who has shown difficulty in reading might be asked to make an oral presentation on who might win the NBA Championship, Super Bowl or World Series after reviewing and analyzing newspaper stories on certain professional sports teams and developing his own logical conclusions.

- allowing students to watch television programs they normally watch, even though such programs may be considered negative. Students can write a paper on what makes such programs inappropriate and what negative values those programs impart.

- giving students assignments that require viewing more documentaries, educational programs, and programs dealing with current issues.

## 8) Communicate so that Your Real Intentions Are Understood

Cross-cultural miscommunication in the classroom does exist. Such miscommunication can lead to lower motivation and lower achievement, excessive speech/language therapy placements, perceptions of frequent, if unintentional, social insults from teachers and other students, frequent misunderstandings and misinterpretations from school personnel and other students, perception of negative school climate, and poor performance on tests and assessments.[12]

Teachers can avoid the consequences of cultural miscommunication through use of the following suggestions:

Become a more effective listener by keeping an open, curious mind; focus on the speaker's ideas while listening with feeling and intuition; become personally involved in what students say; ask for clarification when something is unclear; and listen to the essence of what's said.

Communication is conveyed from *total* person to *total* person. When we communicate, only 7% of what is conveyed comes from our words. 38% is non-verbal, through rate of speaking, tone and volume. 55% is non-vocal, through eye contact, body language, and posture.[13] Do not make the mistake of using negative body language; e.g., folded arms across the chest, inattentive eyes, clenched jaw, scowls, etc., when you're trying to send a positive message.

Help students to develop strong eye contact by having warm, encouraging eyes yourself. You may want to use an activity to strengthen eye contact. Allow students to work in small groups where they will cut out pairs of human eyes taken from magazines, articles, etc. Have them label what each set of eyes means; friendly eyes, fearless eyes, etc. Put some of these labeled eyes on a bulletin board. Students will be able to "look into eyes" throughout the day. This will become a habit-forming practice of looking into eyes. Believe me, it works!

## 9) Establishing a Good School and Classroom Climate

The climate of the classroom is the key to keeping students excited and motivated. There are climate variables that experts know affect behavior between students and teachers. The "climate" should not only welcome students but also keep them encouraged. In Chapter Six, more specific strategies are offered on creating a climate most conducive to achievement by Black and Hispanic students.

## 10) Strengthen Relations Between the Home and School

Most experts have concluded that the involvement of parents in the education of their children is essential to long-term school success.[14] However, many teachers do very little to encourage parental involvement and support. It should be emphasized that many parents simply do not know what they are "supposed" to be doing to enhance their child's academic self-image. Many have been socialized to believe that education is strictly the teacher's domain and that very little is required of them as parents. Teachers must reach out to parents and guardians and make them feel comfortable about the role they will play as equal partners in the education of their children. More specific strategies on strengthening this delicate bond will be shared in Chapter Seven.

These tips will work only if teachers *believe* they can make a difference. Half-hearted, lackluster implementation of any of these strategies will result only in failure. Even when these steps are followed enthusiastically, however, some teachers still may not meet with *immediate* success. All educators must remember that the same persistence we encourage in students *must* be used by school officials as well. Once these tips are put into practice, student discipline may be less problematic. The chapters that follow provide additional insight on creating the most conducive environment for good student behavior, student success, *and* teacher gratification.

# Notes

1. Glasgow, D. *The Black Underclass: Poverty, Unemployment and Entrapment of Ghetto Youth*. San Francisco: Josset Bass Limited, 1980.

2. Fagan, J. and Jones, S.J. "Toward A Theoretical Model for Intervention with Violent Juvenile Offenders" in *Violent Youth Offenders*, Robert Mathias editor. San Francisco: National Council on Crime and Delinquency, CA 1984.

3. Kuykendall, C. *Improving Black Student Achievement by Enhancing Student Self-Image*. Washington, D.C.: Mid-Atlantic Equity Center, American University, 1989.

4. Howard, B. *Learning To Persist, Persisting To Learn*. Washington, D.C.: Mid-Atlantic Equality Center, 1987, American University.

5. Marks, W. *Strategies for Educational Change: Recognizing the Gifts and Talents of All Children*. New York: McMillan Publishing Co., 1981.

6. Fordham, S. and Ozbu, J. "Black Students' School Success: Coping with the Burden of Acting White." *The Urban Review,* Vol. 18, No. 3, 1986.

7. Beane, D. *Mathematics and Science: Critical Fillers for the Future of Minority Students*. Washington, D.C.: Mid-Atlantic Center for Race Equity, American University, 1988.

8. Howard, B. Op. Cit.

9. Fordham, S. and Ozbu, J. Op. Cit.

10. Gilbert, S. and Gay, G. "Improving The Success In School of Poor Black Children." *Phi Delta Kappen,* October 1985.

11. Kuykendall, C. *You and Yours: Making The Most of This School Year*, Washington, D.C.: Mid-Atlantic Equity Center of American University, 1987.

12. Taylor, Orlando, *Cross-Cultural Communication: An Essential Dimension of Effective Education.* Washington, D.C.: Mid-Atlantic Equality Center of American University, 1987.

13. Weinberg, G. and Catero. H. *How to Read A Person Like A Book*, New York: Hawthorn Books, 1971.

14. Henderson, A., "The Evidence Continues to Grow: Parent Involvement Improves Student Achievement," Columbia, MD: NCCE, 1987.

# 5  ADDRESSING THE NEED FOR DISCIPLINE

*As the twig is bent, so the tree is inclined...*

Anonymous

There is a need for effective classroom management. There is also a commensurate need to help students overcome obstacles to self-control and good self-discipline. While "good behavior" is necessary for all students to realize achievement gains, teachers have a better chance of increasing achievement motivation when they can develop in students the sense of responsibility, self-control, and the desire to achieve lifelong success.

The two basic causes of poor student behavior are internal—within the schools—and external—through family, peers, cultural influences, and other factors outside of the school.

## Internal Causes of Poor Student Discipline

If a student feels unwelcome or like an intruder, that student may demonstrate the need to be an integral part of the class through disruptive behavior. This desire for inclusion calls attention to the dominant need of the student for recognition.

Quite often, disruptive students are responding to what *they* perceive as the teacher's belief in the student's inferiority. In such cases, students are likely to react with negative behavior that actually puts them in control of what happens in class. Similarly, some students satisfy their need for recognition, acceptance, appreciation, and inclusion by engaging in behavior that appears to be courting the rejection of the classroom teacher. Teachers should understand that many of these "hostile" and disruptive youth actually fear emotional slights from teachers. They may put up a hypersensitive defensive front to protect their feelings and emotions.

While it is true that some disruptive Black and Hispanic students are simply bored or restless, many are responding to or ventilating the rage they feel as a result of their loss of hope and their likely school failure. When schools fail to prepare youth for lifelong success, they are inviting trouble. A truly "hopeless" child is likely to be a real "problem" child as well. To augment the hope Black and Hispanic students need, teachers and schools must avoid institutional policies and programs such as tracking or ability grouping, which send signals of inferiority. Students are commonly placed in special education classes when it is the students' behavior rather than their ability that causes problems. This practice must be avoided if we are to help these students.

Many students are also likely to respond negatively to what they may perceive as unequal or unfair treatment. Selective rule enforcement, where some students are disciplined and other students are "excused" for committing the same infraction must be eradicated altogether.

The self-fulfilling prophecy about behavior still holds true in our schools. It is important that teachers don't communicate preconceived notions about behavioral tendencies or suggest that students are "bad," "uncouth," or more likely to misbehave than other students. If they do, the students are likely to behave accordingly.

The failure to provide students with frequent opportunities for success and accomplishment in the classroom is another contributing factor to poor behavior. Black and Hispanic students have a need to show what they can do, just as other students take pride in showing their work. If students are not given frequent opportunities for success through classroom activities, they are likely to satisfy the need for accomplishment by telling jokes or disrupting class.

## External Causes of Poor Student Discipline

External causes of poor student discipline are rooted in family and cultural influences and the negative influence of peers.

While most teachers expect that parents will play a major role in disciplining their child, there are some parents who are unable to instill the values or develop the character requisite for appropriate school behavior. Some of these parents even have "given up" on their own children. Does this mean the schools should give up, too?

Some families actually reward children—or give tacit approval—to behavior that the school might find unacceptable. For example, some youth may come from homes where parents encourage speaking out, telling jokes, questioning rules, fighting back, or laughing out loud. In such instances, we cannot blame children for their lack of awareness of the cultural and communication norms which are valued by our educational institutions. We must help them to understand and appreciate appropriate behavioral norms without giving the impression that we are demanding "conformity" or that we dislike them because of their behavior. In addition, "parent awareness" conferences can take place between school officials and parents to make certain parents understand acceptable and unacceptable behavior.

Peer groups obviously play a big role in mitigating or enhancing behavioral problems. As noted previously, many youth develop an "us versus them" mentality when they think the school has already rejected them. These students feel that the only support they have comes from peers who see teachers as "the enemy." Schools must break down this alienation or discipline problems will continue. Teachers can influence students and their rebellious peer groups through strategies designed to reflect genuine concern, support, and some under-standing.

## Strategies for Discipline Problems

There have been numerous suggestions throughout this book for enhancing student self-image and motivation. How-ever, there are many other things teachers can do. Teachers must first check their own attitudes and motivations, incorpo-rate classroom strategies with the greatest likelihood of reduc-ing discipline problems, and use appropriate activities and strategies once poor behavior surfaces.

*Checking Your Attitude.* While it may be hard to be-lieve, there are actually some teachers who *don't like* certain children. This dislike comes across not only to that student, but to other students as well. Teachers who find it difficult to like a particular child should seek instead to love the "human-ity" in that child. If the teacher cannot "love" the child's hu-manity, that teacher should question whether or not he or she belongs in this profession.

Marva Collins suggests telling some poorly disciplined children—on a daily basis—what you like about them and seeking to discern what they like about themselves.[1] When students know there is a bond of genuine admiration and appreciation, they are more receptive to suggestions from the teacher regarding behavior which might be changed. Once adequate bonding has occurred, teachers can get students to discuss behavior they would like to change or improve in themselves.

Teachers also should develop the attitudes that *there are no "bad children,"* just *"inappropriate behavior."* I recall that when I was a young and sometimes quite mischievous child, my mother would remind me of her intense love for me, even when she was acknowledging her strong dislike for inappro-priate behavior. I continued to do this as a parent and teacher.

Teachers will be unable to implement strategies and activities which will prevent student misbehavior if they believe:

- most Black and Hispanic youth are just "bad kids."

- a "good" student is a "quiet" student.

- a "good" class is a class where there is no active learning, no movement, or student interaction.

- students learn best when there is no class noise.

- children are being disrespectful when they challenge a teacher's fairness.

- all youth who crack jokes, laugh loudly, or show nonconformity in dress, personal appearance, or dialect are inherently underachievers.

***Using "Preventive Strategies".*** Once students get the message that *their* education and lifelong success is the *school's* priority, they are more likely to respond with favorable and positive behavior. This message is conveyed through the effective use of teaching styles that have a positive impact on student motivation. As they exist now, many schools and classrooms are not structured to facilitate the achievement of many Black and Hispanic students. Classrooms are still predominantly "teacher centered" as opposed to "student centered." Many teachers still engage in behavior which suggests they are impersonal, aloof, and uncomfortable with the existence of diverse populations in their schools. Even in some all-Black schools, some Black teachers have been known to behave towards some of their lower-class students in ways that suggest the student is not wanted. As indicated previously, student reaction to perceived indifference is predictably negative.

The following additional suggestions will help teachers to deter students from becoming discipline problems:

Make certain you have taken time with the student to discuss *one-on-one* the student's lifelong goals and how the experience in *your* class will help facilitate fulfillment of that lifelong goal. If you have not already used the "Success Chart" presented in Table V, plan to do so immediately with a student who is prone to "acting up."

Plan to build on the non-academic strengths of every student. If a student is overly aggressive, make him a class "leader." Give him or her some kind of responsibility for maintaining and generating the cooperation of other students in class activities. If you have a real "clown" on your hands, give him a daily assignment to start or end the class with a humorous act that will also share a *positive* message. Remember, all children have a special gift or talent. Creative and effective teachers are able to augment student motivation by providing opportunities for each of these "gifted" students to shine. In so doing, these teachers are able to offset the negative actions of children who are seeking recognition in the class.

Provide opportunities for success and accomplishment. Black and Hispanic students are more likely to engage in non-conformist, deviant classroom behavior when they are not given opportunities to succeed at *something*. Teachers should assign class projects for potentially disruptive youth that not only build on that child's individual and cultural strengths but which will satisfy the need for success. For example, students can be asked to complete an assignment that calls for them to describe their own experiences and contrast them with the experiences of other students. Students might also be given an assignment which calls for them to respond to open-ended questions, such as "what do you think would have happened if...." Such an activity will not only provide an opportunity for successful completion, it also will enhance the critical-thinking skills of the student.

Enhance responsibility by giving students a role to play in maintaining a "manageable" classroom. Many students are unmotivated and disruptive because of teacher behavior that stresses adult domination and student obedience.[2] According to research by McClelland, adult domination occurs when adults prescribe what a youth is to do and how it is to be done.

McClelland also concluded that adults who stress obedience and conformity in order to develop "polite and manageable" children inadvertently lower achievement motivation.[3]

Teachers can enhance the clarification of positive values and improve responsible behavior in Black and Hispanic students by making them a part of the rule-enforcement process. Teachers can divide students into small work groups and give each group the task of determining, *as a group*, ten rules that should govern all classroom behavior. Each group also must agree on appropriate consequences for rule violations. Each small group then presents to the whole class the rules and consequences they developed. It would be helpful if students were provided with newsprint and markers to record their decisions.

Once every group has presented its consensus determination on appropriate rules and the reasons *why* they felt these rules should be enforced, the class votes on the rules and consequences by which they will be governed. One complete list of rules and consequences is then placed in a prominent place in the classroom for everyone to see.

This activity will improve student behavior by giving them a feeling of "ownership" for the structure and operation of the classroom. More importantly, this activity also will enhance the students' sense of responsibility, their acceptance of positive values and behavioral norms, and the cohesion among students in the classroom. Children are more likely to support and encourage other children when they share responsibility, purpose, and common values.

Show students your respect for them individually and collectively. Some teachers resort to behavior that belittles, demeans, and destroys student bonding and self-confidence when they are confronted with inappropriate student behavior. The disrespect of these teachers for their students is demonstrated through unnecessarily harsh tones, a denial of student requests for assistance, nonverbal body language, superior attitudes, and unequal enforcement of rules. In most children's programs, it does not take long to see that adults expect to be treated with more respect than they demonstrate.[4]

Establish trusting relationships with students. Marva Collins suggests making friends with students, complimenting them, letting them know how much they were missed when they have been absent, and even sitting with them during lunch.[5] Teachers also can take time to discuss with students any real or perceived problems that student may be having at home, in the school (with other teachers or students), or in other environments.

## What to Do When They Still Misbehave

Even when a teacher feels he has been supportive, respectful, and caring, students may still behave "inappropriately." Teachers should understand that many Black and Hispanic youth often are socialized with attitudes and strategies designed to enhance their survival in a White environment that is more often than not perceived to be hostile. These students are taught to appreciate some skills and behavioral norms that are not always condoned in our classrooms. Some of those skills that may be prized in their respective communities, but not in our schools, include nonverbal communication, dance and rhythmic movements, rapping, learning through cooperative dependence on others, and verbal interplay during instruction.

Teachers must still socialize Black and Hispanic students to live both inside and outside of their own cultural groups. However, teachers risk further alienation when they refuse to understand or appreciate the cultural values, norms, and communication patterns these youth bring to the learning environment.

Even when students behave inappropriately, teachers may be able to use adverse behavior as an opportunity to facilitate student growth and acceptance of corrective behavioral norms. The following tips should help:

***Punish the Behavior—Not the Person.*** It is important that this distinction be made. Teachers must inform students constantly—through spoken and written reminders and supportive behavior—that they respect and admire them as individuals. Once students understand that the consequences are for inappropriate behavior rather than the students' existence, they are more likely to modify the behavior and to accept the guidance of well-meaning adults.

***Discipline Students with a Firm but "Loving Touch."*** If there is no love, no genuine concern, no desire to help, the disciplinary act is likely to lead to bitterness and resentment, not maturity.[6] Renowned educator Marva Collins offers the following guideposts for dealing with disruptive students:[7]

- Have students write compositions or deliver three-minute speeches on the etymology of gum, rather than punitive lines such as, "I will not chew gum in class."

- Continue to reward and compliment them for good behavior and take extra teaching time, either before or after school, to help students who are slower and more likely to misbehave.

***Use Creative Alternatives to Suspension, Detention and Isolation.*** Many school districts use alternative suspension programs, or "in-school" suspension. Quite often, however, even these well-meaning alternatives defeat their purpose. In many in-school suspension programs, students simply go to a room with other "disruptive" students and a "caretaker" adult where they are allowed to do everything *other than learn* from their behavior.

In such "alternative suspension" programs, students should be asked to prepare papers on the impact of their behavior on other students, how their behavior has detracted from their pursuit of legitimate lifelong goals, or how a modification of behavior might make them better people. Most importantly, students should be disciplined in such a way that they do not distance themselves totally from the learning process.

Many times, students who exhibit inappropriate behavior are retained, put out of the class, or put into special education classes. Unless they are given opportunities to assess the impact of their behavior and to analyze reasons for behavioral change, such practices will do more harm than good.

Teachers will always be faced with mischievous and disruptive students. Even when students display a mischievous streak, however, they still deserve opportunities for transformation and academic growth. A good teacher can make certain such opportunities are always a part of the school day.

Finally, teachers must make effective use of climate variables that affect student behavior and student attitudes toward self. These climate variables, and the need for an environment that is more conducive to learning and more encouraging school buildings, are discussed in the next chapter.

# Notes

1. Collins, M. *Marva Collins' Way*. Los Angles: Jeremy P. Tarcher, Inc., 1990.

2. McClelland, D. "Sources of An Achievement" in McClelland, D. and Stelle, R. (editors) *Human Motivation*. Morristown, NJ: General Learning Press, 1973. Taken from Brendtro, L., Brokenleg, M. and Van Dochern, S. *Reclaiming Youth at Risk*. Bloomington, IN: National Educational Service, 1990.

3. Ibid.

4. Brendtro, L., Brokenleg, M. and Van Bochern, S. *Reclaiming Youth At-Risk*. Bloomington, IN: National Educational Service, 1990.

5. Collins, M. op. cit.

6. Ibid.

7. Ibid.

# 6 CREATING A GOOD SCHOOL AND CLASSROOM CLIMATE

*I have come to a frightening conclusion that I am the decisive element in the classroom. It is my personal approach that creates the climate, my daily mood that makes the weather....*

Haim Ginott
*Between Teacher & Child*

Children, especially Black and Hispanic children, respond to their surroundings. Colors evoke certain feelings and emotions in all of us, but colors and other physical trappings have a strong impact on moods and behavior in children. Teachers and administrators must make certain that the classroom and school climate neither stifle growth nor destroy confidence.

However, classroom climate is composed of more than physical appearance. Climate is also influenced by atmosphere and the prevailing conditions affecting activity. Through the school and classroom climate, students are often inspired, nurtured, supported and comforted. A good school climate can generate enthusiasm, clarify values, build confidence, and strengthen relationships. Thus, school and class climate is significant in the motivation of all students, but it is especially significant for Black and Hispanic students.

## Physical Conditions

Children who attend school in dilapidated, antiquated, and poorly kept facilities are likely to feel the psychological effects of inequitable school resources. The push during the 1970's to outlaw intradistrict disparities in school financing was largely a result of the concern administrators and policy-makers were having with the impact of these obvious, and in some cases, blatant disparities.

The first consideration in creating a motivational climate is to make certain the physical facility itself is one of which students can feel proud. If the building does happen to be old and somewhat rundown, insist that the school board make the repairs a priority. Gardening classes, art classes, and landscaping classes also can work with school officials to beautify the outside of the school.

Students who are proud of the physical building itself are at least likely to feel a certain degree of comfort in being at that school. Yet, as we all know, even when the exterior looks great, it's what's on the inside that counts.

## The Internal Climate

The correlates for Effective Schooling include an emphasis on establishing a good school learning climate.[1]

a) The first correlate emphasizes a positive commitment of all staff to student achievement. It is important that individual teachers be committed to *each one* of their students. However, when this commitment exists in *all* adult staff, a climate is established where every student knows he is expected to do well and will not be allowed to be less than his best.

A total school approach to educating Black and Hispanic students must involve all school personnel in the socialization of these youth. Cafeteria workers, custodians, engineers, secretaries, bus drivers, nurses, and other support staff must understand the impact of their behavior and biases on student self-image and motivation. If students or parents feel they are unwelcome, unappreciated, or disrespected, their desire to please and bond with adults in the school is likely to deteriorate.

Not only must individuals in the school communicate their respect, appreciation, and belief in every child, the school itself must convey a positive message of hope. This can be done through the use of bulletin boards, murals, "walls of fame," display boards (for student essays), school slogans, pep rallies (which encourage excellence in all areas), school songs, and other school-spirit activities.

In addition, the school must implement programs that reflect its appreciation of the diverse gifts and talents in all students. In many gifted-and-talented programs, children are identified as gifted only if they show above average cognitive skills. However, Black and Hispanic youth are especially gifted in non-academic areas and should be allowed the opportunity to have those gifts developed as well.

Schools can create the following clubs and programs for youth who show special gifts:

- Comedy Club (for class clowns).

- Current-Issues Debate Team (for excessive talkers).

- Rappers Forum (for poets and "rappers").

- Leaders Forum (for students who may not show academic skills but who are recognized as leaders by their peers).

- "New You" Club (for male and female students whose strength seems to be personal adornment, style, and cosmetology).

- Designers Club (for students interested in designing clothes and fashions).

- Artists Alley (for students who exhibit special skills in art).

- Magic Music Makers Club (for students who play instruments).

- Future Engineers Club (for students with mechanical abilities).

This list is not exhaustive. Take time at your school to discuss the creation of clubs that can strengthen the talents and enhance the gifts of all students.

b) In the previous chapter, I discussed some of the school-related causes of poor student behavior. In establishing appropriate standards of behavior, school policymakers and officials should first convene a task force of parents, teachers, and civic, social, religious, and community leaders to determine what student behaviors are currently inappropriate. Many schools have discipline handbooks or codes that are so outdated they no longer reflect the needs of contemporary school children. In allowing the community to have input on the development of a revised handbook or code, administrators can facilitate development of a "community of caring," where significant community representatives can have a collective influence on student motivation and achievement.

Share with parents the primary concern of the school. Is it motivation/achievement, or is it the maintenance of good student behavior and public relations? Make sure every parent is instructed (perhaps during the first visit with the classroom teacher) on the contents of the Discipline Handbook or the school Code of Conduct. Make certain every classroom teacher takes time to discuss school rules and consequences for violation during class instruction. The distinction should be made about the difference between enforcement of school rules and the development and enforcement of class rules. And, make certain Black and Hispanic students are not disciplined unfairly and are not "singled out" for the poor behavior of an entire class or group.

c) In order to be effective, a school must provide a purposeful, safe and orderly environment. School officials must also rethink the parameters of an "orderly environment." Children should feel safe but should not be made to feel they are in prison. Research on learning styles tells us that there should be more activity, movement, and sharing during some of the learning experiences of Black and Hispanic youth. This means that "order" might, by necessity, be defined as that which fosters student motivation. The school can establish a code that determines hall behavior, bathroom behavior, lunchroom behavior, playground behavior, etc. However, teachers and students should be allowed to establish class rules.

## Class Climate

The learning environment must enhance rather than hurt the academic self-image of students. In so doing, the climate itself can augment motivation and actual achievement. Several factors must be considered in establishing an appropriate learning environment. As with school climate, these factors can be characterized in terms of the physical setting and teacher behaviors.

***The Physical Setting.*** Classrooms must not only be comfortable, they must also create an atmosphere where all students can get excited about their achievement and future goals. Care must be taken by educators to have appropriate lighting, ventilation, and temperatures. In addition, the physical setting should also include such things as:

- colorful decorations with warm, bold colors.

- positive slogans that foster values, keep students inspired, and facilitate persistence.

- information on the accomplishments and contributions of Black and Hispanic leaders, inventors, civil, social, and human rights leaders, and other heroes and heroines. Such a class wall should remain in existence all year, not just in February. In high schools, this wall can feature information and pictures of Blacks who have contributed in the particular subject area (i.e., science,

English, etc.)—as long as there are other walls in the school that reflect contributions of Blacks and Hispanics in all walks of life and professional areas.

- information that reflects facts on particular content areas, and areas that concern integrated content areas.

- displays of individual work and accomplishments. During the year, every child should see something he has done on the wall.

- learning stations where resource materials are available.

The physical setting should also be conducive to student-student interaction and student-teacher interaction. It helps if children are not seated one behind the other and if they have movable chairs. Teachers can facilitate student pride in their classroom by encouraging cleanliness and student ideas on how to"beautify" the learning environment.

A highly decorated classroom *alone* will not keep Black and Hispanic students motivated. The behavior of the teacher is significant in determining how comfortable and excited these students will be in the learning environment.

***Teacher Behavior.*** In previous chapters I emphasized the powerful impact of teacher behavior on student attitudes and behavior. In her assessment of teacher expectations on student achievement, Sheryl Denbo described climate variables as "teacher behaviors which affect student attitudes toward self, and teacher behaviors which build or destroy respect between students and teachers."[2]

Through behavior, teachers should be able to foster:

- mutual trust and respect between students.

- mutual helpfulness between students.

- acceptance of student differences and a multicultural appreciation.

- freedom of student expression.

When teachers are disrespectful to some students, they create a climate where other students feel it's permissible to show disrespect. In a study by Ray Rist, high achieving students in a classroom where students were grouped by ability belittled students labeled as low-achievers—following the model of interaction set by the classroom teacher.[3] Other experts, including Lippit, Good, and Brophy,[4] have commented on the failure of many teachers to set an example that reflects courtesy and respect for youth.

The "us versus them" mentality that exists in many schools, reflecting animosity between low-achieving Black and Hispanic youth and school officials, often carries over to student relationships. If made to feel inferior by other students— who are simply modeling adult behavior—some underachieving students may resort to acts of verbal assault. Similarly, a lack of trust between teachers and students is likely to create a lack of trust between students. The end result—the worst-case scenario—is an "integrated" school where segregation, classism, and elitism still exist. When students are unable to trust one another, or even respect one another, they are unlikely to support one another or develop mutually interdependent relationships, which can foster achievement gains and coexistence in a diverse society.

Teachers should also foster mutual helpfulness. A climate that enhances mutual support, helpfulness, and interdependence is created more easily when teachers use praise and affirmation in communicating with all students, are in closer proximity to low achieving Black and Hispanic students, and use student recommendations to monitor student progress.

Research shows that Black and Hispanic students receive less teacher praise and more teacher criticism than do White students.[5] Even when Blacks and Hispanics give a right answer, those who are perceived as underachievers are still less likely to be praised than students perceived as high achievers.[6] A 1985 study by David & Myra Sadker found that teachers were more likely to say, "O.K.," to Black students than to

White students, whether or not their answer was correct, thus leaving the Black student with little information about the quality of his or her performance.[7] Teachers who continue to display such obvious signs of bias are only encouraging negative interaction among students.

Physical proximity also is important. While there are different cultural perceptions of the need for physical touching and closeness in the classroom, there is an abundance of research indicating that physical closeness, for the most part, is a good teaching technique. Students who are physically closest to the teacher receive more academic and non-academic attention.[8]

Teachers cannot be expected to change their seating charts daily. However, a good teacher will move around the class so that every child feels some proximity. In so doing, teachers send a message to all students that every child is an integral and welcome part of the learning environment. All too often, when teachers are in close proximity to underachieving students, it's to dominate them, discipline them, or to degrade them. When physical closeness conveys a spirit of support and helpfulness, other students are more likely to feel a desire to offer similar help and support.

Student recommendations should be used to monitor student progress. Given what we know about test bias, it is important that educators look at alternative means of monitoring student progress. Students can (and should) be encouraged to participate in non-testing techniques that allow some students to provide teachers with information about what other students are learning.[9] Through the use of the "buddy game," heterogenous grouping/cooperative learning, think-pair-share (where students discuss their analyses with a partner before opening their thoughts up for class discussion), and team projects, students can provide the support and insight to facilitate the achievement gains of others in a positive and helpful manner.

It is very important for teachers to foster acceptance of student differences and multicultural appreciation. As a result of the civil rights movement of the 1960s, there has been more of an effort to educate all students on the accomplishments and contributions of all cultural groups. Few can deny the continued importance of non-biased instructional materials which augment racial/cultural pride and improved race relations. However, while many schools and school systems are moving in this direction, there is still significant resistance. The debate in many urban school districts over whether to incorporate an "Afrocentric" curriculum or a "multicultural curriculum" is an indication that we are still wrestling with how far we should go in our efforts to improve cultural awareness and a celebration of all racial/cultural heritages. The continued used by school officials of words like "minorities" is one indication that we still have far to go.

Although many administrators of Afrocentric educational programs report improved student discipline, there still is no data on the impact of such programs on actual achievement. Yet, improved discipline is a powerful sign that there is an improved desire in students to be a part of the learning experience. Schools can enhance the motivation of youth when they provide a climate where cultural diversity is celebrated, not just in what we teach but also in how we teach. The entire culture of the school must be expanded to accept and celebrate student differences.

Teachers must foster freedom of expression. When students feel uncomfortable about expressing themselves, they are more likely to disengage themselves from the learning process. Teachers can encourage freedom by accepting various means of expression, by being willing to listen, and showing emphatic understanding and an interest in the child as a person.

Some Black and Hispanic students express themselves through poetry, artwork, songs, "rap", dance, or other media. While it is necessary that all students learn how to express themselves in socially acceptable manners, i.e., through the use of standard English in speaking and writing, students should be encouraged to engage in various means of expression which may reflect individual or cultural strengths.

Once students get the message that teachers are unwilling to listen to their concerns or responses, these youth are less likely to express themselves. Remember, good teachers must be able to listen to verbal communication and understand what is communicated through nonverbal behavior.

Many underachieving students feel trapped in schools where teachers and adminstrators just "don't understand" them. Even though some teachers may not know what a child might be internalizing, experiencing, or feeling, teachers can still show a willingness to accept and validate the feelings of that particular child. Children, especially Black and Hispanic children, need to feel that perceived barriers to understanding can be eradicated.

A teacher who shows a desire to understand and some sincerity in accepting student feelings can establish more meaningful bonds with the student. I advocate the use of "feel, felt, found." When students convey feelings of anger, frustration, or hopelessness, teachers can respond by saying, "I know how you feel" or, "I can imagine how you must feel." "I've been in situations where I felt the exact same way, but this is what I found out." The teacher can then share with the student insight on how to make the best of what appears to be a bad situation.

Many students are alienated from schools because of the behavior of a few teachers, counselors, and/or administrators who show no interest in the child or in anything the child feels is important.

Recently, I saw a teacher express outrage when a 14-year-old Black student discussed the significance of his religion with other students. The student happened to be Muslim. He was proud of his religion, race, and family background. Because the teacher responded so negatively to the students' discussion, that student and other students in the class responded by emotionally removing themselves from the learning experience. Teachers should be sensitive to the religious beliefs of *all* their students.

It is important for course relevance that teachers encourage culturally and racially diverse students to express their own experiences and interests in the classroom. Through implementation of these suggestions and the creation of a school and classroom climate that is more conducive to the education and motivation of Black and Hispanic youth, educators are going a step further in strengthening the home-school bond.

# Notes

1.  Hale-Benson, J., *Black Children: Their Roots, Culture and Learning Styles*. Provo, UT: Brigham Young University Press, 1982.

2.  Denbo. *Improving Minority Student Achievement: Focus on the Classroom*. Washington, D.C.: Mid-Atlantic Equity Center of American University, 1986.

3.  Rist, R. "Social Distance and Social Inequality in a Ghetto Kindergarten Classroom." *Urban Education* 7 (October 1972).

4.  Good, T.L., Brophy, J.E., *Looking In Classrooms*, New York: Harper & Row Publishers, 1973 and Lippit, R. and Others. *An Inter-Center Program for Studies in Children, Youth and Family Life of the Survey Research Center and the Research Center for Group Dynamics*, Ann Arbor, MI: University of Michigan, n.d., taken from Denbo, S., Ibid.

5.  Dunken, M.J. and Biddle, B.J. *The Study of Teaching*. New York: Holt, Rinehart & Winston, 1974.

6.  Good, T.L., Brophy, J.E., op. cit.

7.  Sadker, D. and Sadker, M. "Is the O.K. Classroom O.K.?" Taken from Denbo, S., op. cit. *Phi Delta Kappan* 66 (January 1985).

8.  Denbo, S. op. cit.

9.  Lezotte, L.W. and Bancroft, B.A. "School Improvement Based on Effective Schools Research: A Promising Approach for Economically Disadvantaged Minority Students." *Journal of New Education* 54, Summer 1985. Taken from Denbo, S. op. cit.

# 7 STRENGTHENING THE HOME-SCHOOL BOND

*...the family structure and cultural backgrounds of children in school seem to be becoming ever more diverse and complex, and...educators are understandably uneasy and perplexed about what these changes mean for children, for parents, and for the schools they are expected to run. In spite of the difficulties that family-school partnerships may entail, working together is critically important for students..."*

From *Beyond the Bake Sale:*
*An Educator's Guide to Working With Parents*
by Ann T. Henderson,
Carl L. Marburger,
Theodora Oams

The positive impact of parental involvement on the achievement motivation of students has been well-documented.[1] Yet, as vital as parental involvement is to student achievement, as important as it is for schools themselves, many parents do much less than they should and many schools engage in practices which only serve to limit the extent of parental involvement in school decision-making available to diverse cultural groups.

Parental involvement is vital to the achievement of students. Unfortunately, many parents are doing much less than they should be doing. Research indicates that on average, American mothers spend less than half an hour a day talking, explaining, or reading with their children. Fathers spend less than 15 minutes.[2] In addition, many schools give only lip service and tacit approval to parental involvement while imposing barriers that keep parents—especially Black and Hispanic parents—away.

The partnership between home and schools is so very important that educators and administrators must take immediate steps to strengthen it. The one marriage that must work—for the sake of the children—is the marriage between home and school. Therefore, schools must get more Black and Hispanic parents involved; schools must keep Black and Hispanic parents excited; and they must use and strengthen other community resources and social systems.

Parents can be educated to play significant roles in the school decision-making process. Unfortunately, many educators, administrators, and policymakers want to limit parental involvement. They see parents' role as one they should play at home, fostering achievement gains for their *own* children. The partnership between home and schools is so *very* important that educators and administrators must take immediate steps to strengthen it. This chapter will address:

- what parental involvement *is* and should be.

- how to get Black and Hispanic parents more involved.

- how to keep Black and Hispanic parents excited.

- how to use and strengthen other community resources and social systems.

## What Is Parental Involvement?

Parents can be educated to play significant roles in the school decision making process through their individual and organizational endeavors. Many parents who were participants in the Citizens Training Institute of the National Committee for Citizens in Education under my direction from 1975-78 have since become school board members, city council representatives, and educators. Schools can still help parents obtain the insight and understanding needed to be advocates for school success. However schools must convey these positive and encouraging thoughts so that parents can feel a need for better partnerships.

Educators are realizing now that parental involvement *must* mean more than helping the child at home. Certainly schools should encourage parents to help children with homework and develop in them good manners and discipline. Parents should be encouraged to give children good and nourishing breakfasts, keep them inspired, read to them, talk to them, etc. However, the involvement of Black and Hispanic parents must include more than PTA membership, back sales, and "at home" assistance. Educators also must involve them in the following areas as:

- classroom tutors, helpers and field trip volunteers.

- members of a local school decision making team.

- members of the school district's salary committee.

- members of the school district's curriculum development committee.

- members of the district's disciplinary committee.

- members of the principal selection committee.

- members of the school or district budget committee.

- members of a school design committee.

- participants in teacher contract negotiations.

Some states do have legislation that calls for parental involvement in some of these areas. School officials might be surprised to discover that such extensive involvement by Black and Hispanic parents will only improve student achievement.

Once school officials expand their definitions of what constitutes "effective parental involvement," they also can develop strategies that will get parents involved at every conceivable level. However, involving Black and Hispanic parents requires more than an expanded definition, it requires carefully developed strategies for getting and keeping parents excited about the school process. Educators first must *believe* that the involvement of Black and Hispanic parents is needed for the school to succeed.

## How to Get Black and Hispanic Parents Involved

Many Black and Hispanic parents are likely to be more involved in school activities when their children are in the preschool and primary grades. Nevertheless, an intense level of involvement is needed in the intermediate grades, where the classroom environment is less socially interactive and more competitive and individualistic.[3] There has already been a discussion of the drop in self-image among Black youth between first and fifth grades. Some observers have even expressed alarm over a "fourth grade failure syndrome" among Black boys.[4]

Teachers should assume a greater professional responsibility by taking the initiative in enlisting parental involvement at every grade level. The following are suggestions of what good teachers and administrators *can* do to encourage participation of Black and Hispanic parents.

### Make Certain Your Attitude is a Positive One

To enlist parental support, teachers and administrators should make certain that their "attitude" is positive. Many Black and Hispanic parents to whom I've spoken have expressed dismay over the condescending and pedantic tone of some classroom teachers. It's important that educators refrain from using demeaning and degrading words to describe family structures. Words such as "dysfunctional families" suggest to some Black and Hispanic students and parents that their family is inferior. Such words also convey a reluctance to accept the inherent strengths of families in diverse cultures. Some would be surprised to learn of the tremendous strength that exists in many non-nuclear, but "extended" Black and Hispanic families.

Teachers should take time to understand the dynamics of these powerful extended families. Some Black families derive so much from extended family relations that even the terminology used to describe family members is different. For example, my sister, brother, and I follow an African tradition that does not recognize words like "aunt," "uncle," "cousin," "niece," or "nephew". The children of both my brother and sister refer to me as "Mommy," and they refer to each other as brother and sister. Dysfunctional? Quite the contrary!

In addition, many "single parent" families among Black and Hispanics are still supported by an extended network so that single mothers are not raising children "singly."[5] The continued use of terms which reflect institutionalized disrespect for Black and Hispanic lifestyles only fosters alienation. Once teachers are able to see Black and Hispanic parents as capable individuals who deserve respect, they are more likely to make the overtures necessary to enhance the home-school partnership.

## Make the First Contact with the Parent a Positive One

Educators must take pains to make the first contact with the parent a positive one. Black and Hispanic parents—like most other Americans—have spent *some* time as students in our nation's schools. Some may still harbor memories of negative school experiences and a few teachers they felt were demeaning and disrespectful. Many of these parents actually fear for their own children.

The excessive suspensions, failures, and placements of Black youth, especially boys, in special education classes supports the belief held by many Black parents that there is, in fact, a conspiracy to destroy Black boys.[6] Some teachers may inadvertently advance that belief when they do not build on the strengths of their Black and Hispanic students. It is the teachers' identification and acceptance of these strengths that can arouse the desire of some parents to build meaningful and cooperative relationships with school personnel.

Rather than make contact with the home when the student has done something wrong, teachers should call parents early in the school year to share some "good news" and favorable anticipation. The suggested conversation below will take only a few minutes, but it will strengthen considerably the parents' resolve to work closely with the school:

**Teacher:**

Hello, I'd like to speak to the parent or guardian of
_____. (Child's Name)

(Once the parent or guardian is on the line):

I am so glad to have a chance to talk to you. I am _____
_____, (Your Name) your child's _____
_____ (Grade or Subject) teacher. I know you're probably busy. I just wanted to take these few minutes to let you know how delighted I am to have _____ (Child's Name) in my class. Already I have noticed his/her _____, (Strength) his/her _____, (Strength) and his/her _____ (Strength). I am looking forward to meeting you so that we can discuss how we might work together to bring out the very best in _____. (Child's Name)

Many parents will be so shocked to receive such a positive call from an obviously sincere and caring teacher that they will not say anything. Some will get off the phone and turn to that child and let him or her know that this teacher is *not* to be given a hard time. I have had teachers who have tried this conversation report to me that many parents have cried—they were so moved by the teacher's show of concern.

During the first face-to-face visit with the parent, teachers should discuss the individual strengths and interests of the child. They should also seek to discern any sensitivities or special qualities that child may have:

- "What have you noticed about Keisha that you consider outstanding?"

- "What kind of things does Rasheki like doing the most?"

- "What activities do you and Antar engage in at home?"

- "How many siblings are there to help Manuel at home?"

- "What has been Eli's previous experience with school?"

- "What kind of personality does Ellen show at home?"

- "Are there any talents Maria has which I should help her to develop?"

- "Are there things I should avoid saying or doing with Kashif?"

Keep in mind—many Black and Hispanic parents are dealing with the day-to-day reality of their own survival. Some will avoid contact with the school if such contact brings only more "bad news".

In addition to the suggestions above, teachers also can maintain contact with parents through notes or calls—especially when there is more good news to report. Teachers also should constantly remind parents that they are *welcome* partners—worthy of the school's utmost respect.

### Don't Be Hypocritical

Some teachers say positive things about students when they talk to parents but maintain a negative attitude when interacting with the student during regular school hours. Some even write negative things in the child's cumulative folder—even after sharing positive things with the parents. Eventually, parents will discover this hypocrisy, and it will make them more reluctant to establish meaningful relations with other school personnel.

### Push for More Parent Education Classes in Your School or District

Parent education classes can be very helpful. There may be a big gulf between what the teacher expects of parents and what the parent feels is expected of him or her. Parent educa-

tion classes can be held to help parents understand such
things as:

- how to develop positive values and character in children.

- the school's mission, objectives, and rules.

- how to develop a "home curriculum" that provides for
  after-school learning enrichments, more parent-student
  interaction and discussion of school obstacles and mile-
  stones.[7]

- what the school expects of both parent and child, and
  what the school is offering in return.

- what the parents' recourse is if their child is suspended,
  placed in special education, or disciplined unfairly.

- who the key players in the school are (e.g. assistant
  principal, nurse, librarian, coach, etc.).

Sharing information builds trust and strengthens the
home-school bond. Some educators and administrators with-
hold information from parents—thereby creating suspicion
and distrust. Make sure your school isn't guilty of turning
away those parent partners so necessary for school success.[8]
Below is a list of replies which have been used by school
officials to keep information from parents, organized groups
and community representatives.[9]

- "We will have you investigated"—threats and intimidation.

- "United we stand"—organized resistance.

- "The information may be harmful and misinter-
  preted"—professional paternalism.

- "You can get it elsewhere"—the dodge.

- "Come and get it"—the invitation.

- "Tell us why you want it first"—limited rights.

- "The law doesn't apply to me"—the exceptionalist argument.

- "It's too much trouble"—administrative burden.

- "Your request is too vague"—contrived confusion.

- "$3.00 per page, please"—the sting.

- "Maybe they'll go away"—the stall.

- "So sue me"—the dare.

- ". . . . . . . . ."—stonewalling.

## Plan a "Family Night" at Your School

A Family Night involves all students and their families in entertainment and fun activities. This special night should be well advertised. Parents should be contacted through flyers and by telephone. Prizes can be awarded to classrooms getting the best parent attendance. This night should be a celebration of everything that makes the school and its students, the parents, and the community so unique and special.

## Encourage Parents to Join Groups and Organizations

Another successful way to get parents involved is to encourage them to join established groups or to start their own organizations. Many Black and Hispanic parents can benefit tremendously from organized involvement with other parents in the school. Established groups can monitor school activities and facilitate overall school improvement. They should *not* be feared by teachers or administrators who want to discourage such parent participation.

Once school officials have gotten parents out and involved, it's important to maintain their excitement and participation. For many educators, however, sustaining parental involvement and support is easier said than done.

## How to Keep Parents Excited

There are several explanations for waning excitement and involvement of some Black and Hispanic parents at intermediate, junior high, and high school levels. All too often, parents lose interest because their children have lost interest.

I know of numerous Black, Hispanic, Native American, and even White parents who see some schools as insensitive, disinterested, punitive, and uncommitted. One parent, whose child had a B average until he reached junior high school, lamented,"It's almost as though they just don't *want* to see him make it." I don't believe the majority of schools are this way. Yet, it's important that educators don't create even an appearance of indifference.

There may be logistical barriers as well. For many Black and Hispanic parents, transportation and child care are obstacles. If a child is bused to a school far from his neighborhood, it may be extremely difficult for parents to take part in school functions or to be a visible presence in the schools. Administrators and teachers must take steps to provide transportation—or meet the parent half way. Also, school functions for parents should encourage *family* participation. Activities can be planned in kindergarten classrooms for smaller children, while parents and older children visit classrooms and partake of other activities. Child care should not be a factor in maintaining parent support.

The scheduling of school activities is also a concern. In some neighborhoods where there is high unemployment (leaving many parents at home during the day), high crime, and poorly lit streets, it may be advisable to have some school functions during the day. Certainly, Saturday and evening events may be best for working parents. Through collaboration with parents and community, teachers and school officials can determine appropriate times for school activities to be planned during the year.

If school officials are able to exhibit more concern and follow many of the suggestions outlined in previous chapters, they will see more parent participation and support. However, good schools will go a step further. These schools will seek to create a "community of caring" where the entire school community is involved in facilitating student success.

# Make Use of Other Community Resources

No school is an island; all schools serve the interests of the communities in which they are located. For this reason, partnerships with the community improve school effectiveness. Unfortunately, there are some school officials who see low-income communities as part of the problem.[10]

There are many appropriate resources within all communities that can be harnessed and used effectively to augment student achievement and school improvement. Educators can make best use of community resources by:

- creating "Blue Ribbon" community panels.

- recruiting and using community businesses.

- making use of other social systems in the community.

## Creating Blue Ribbon Community Panels

School administrators should seek the assistance of school board representatives, other elected officials, parents, and students in identifying community leaders for a "Blue Ribbon" community panel. If there are neighborhood law enforcement officials—or an "Officer Friendly" who walks the "beat" in the community—they also should be invited to participate in such a panel. Such involvement becomes a two-way street—law enforcement officials can share information and also learn more about the youth in their communities.

The "Blue Ribbon" community panel can meet with the principal, students, and parents regularly. There are many things such a panel can do for the school, including:

- sharing insight on how to revise discipline codes.

- sharing insight on other community agencies and resources.

- providing feedback on planned school functions and activities.

- sharing insight on other challenges facing the community so all can be effective trouble-shooters.

- being a part of a school "Wall of Fame" where accomplished community leaders and former graduates of that school are featured and acknowledged.

- showing a united commitment to the success of every child in that school.

Through such a panel, administrators and teachers can identify role models and mentors who can work with students to keep them motivated.

## Recruiting Community Role Models and Mentors

The job of educating youth should be shared by *all* concerned citizens. Every community has residents who can be exemplary role models to youth. The school must take the initiative in reaching out to these potential mentors and providing the leadership for their use in the schools and in classrooms.

Our Black and Hispanic male youth are in particular need of strong role models who can help them to see themselves in the most positive light. School teachers in this country are overwhelmingly White, middle-class, and female. The pool of Black and Hispanic male teachers is dwindling.

Kenneth Jones found that as Black males approach early adulthood, guidance from older Black men is critical. Negative realities or myths regarding the Black community (high unemployment, dropout rates, inclinations toward antisocial behavior, etc.) can be offset by good role models.[11] Rather than leave the development of Black and Hispanic males solely to the schools, peer groups, or *chance*,[12] schools can respond to the need of their male and female students for guidance by enlisting the support of volunteer mentors who provide assistants through efforts to:

- help youth become more responsible.

- help youth set short and long term goals.

- help youth to correct behavior which can alter their lives.

- help youth break down perceived and actual barriers to school success.

- help students to improve in academic areas where they are weakest.

- improve youth discipline and motivation by being a *real* example of what can be done with a purpose and a plan

- help youth develop better bonds with others in the community so that as they become adults, they too will be able to "give something back."[13]

If they seek the assistance of respected role models in the community, school officials will discover there are some very committed individuals who will devote a few hours a week to develop personal bonds with students. As Akbar noted, these bonds can facilitate the exodus of boys into manhood.[14]

## Create Partnerships with Community Businesses

School officials also should encourage private businesses, hospitals, or other public-service institutions to "adopt" their school. Remember, businesses do have a stake in the education and the socialization of students. Whether businesses or institutions actually adopt a school or not, they can still be encouraged to:

- provide resources (paper, school supplies, equipment, furniture, etc.).

- have a representative serve as the school liaison who has a visible presence in the school on a weekly basis.

- have a representative teach or lecture to a class or student body on how to succeed in business.

- arrange for field trips to larger companies or industries within the city.

- provide incentive rewards to students for good attendance, creativity, business plans, or improved achievement.

- assist students or classes with special projects designed to improve math or business skills.

## Use Other Social Systems in the Community

In addition to businesses, most communities have some sort of government-sponsored recreation center, Boys or Girls Clubs, and religious institutions. In Black communities, the Black church is a powerful social institution and should be seen as a partner in the development of young minds. School officials should make a list of resource organizations and institutions serving children in the school community. These organizations may be able to identify mentors or share information on after-school programs that can serve the needs of children for constructive after-school activities.

Educating and preparing all students for life and success in this society is not easy. Yet, it need not be as difficult as some educators have made it. If effective use is made of home and community resources, success can be realized. Now, let's put it all together and focus on *our* future survival.

# Notes

1. Henderson, A., *The Evidence Continues to Grow: Parent Involvement Improves Student Achievement*. Columbia, MD: NCCE, 1987.

2. U.S. Department of Education. *What Works: Research about Teaching and Learning* 1987.

3. Morgan, H."How Schools Fail Black Children." *Social Policy*, Jan-Feb 1980.

4. Ibid.

5. Ibid.

6. Ibid.

7. Walberg, H. "Families As Partners in Educational Productivity." *Phi Delta Kappa*, Feb. 1984.

8. Massachusetts Advocacy Center. "State Report: Freedom of Information in Massachusetts." Boston, MA, March 1975. Taken from Kuykendall, op. cit.

9. Ibid.

10. Kuykendall, C. "A Study of the Responses of Over 2000 Teachers on Needs and Attitudes, 1984-1987" in Washington, DC.

11. Jones, K. "The Black Male in Jeopardy." *The Crisis*, 1986, v. 93 n. 3.

12. Perkins, Useni Eugene. *Home is a Dirty Street: The Social Oppression of Black Children*. Chicago, IL: Third World Press, 1975.

13. Collins, M. *Marva Collins' Way*. Los Angeles: Jeremy P. Tarcher, Inc., 1990.

14. Akbar, N. *Visions for Black Men*. Nashville: Winston Derek Publishers, Inc., 1991.

# 8 FOCUSING ON THE FUTURE

*Nothing in the world helps a man to keep healthy so much as the knowledge of a life task.*

Anonymous

The future is what we make it. Each of us owes it to ourselves and to our children to make certain the future reflects the best contributions of each of us. The time to plan for a secure, promising, and rewarding future is now. Educators have a golden opportunity to mold the future as few other Americans can. As Christa McAuliffe noted, "I am a teacher . . . I touch the future."

Our futures are jeopardized to the extent that we fail as a society to prepare Black and Hispanic students for purposeful and meaningful futures. Too many of these youth have no real concept of *their* futures, and live only for the day or even the moment. The suggestions presented in this book have shown that we are not powerless, and that schools can affect the futures of these students. We, as educators, can foster in them a real dream for a future and the ability to set goals for a lifelong career, occupation, or task. Schools can do what few other institutions can. They *can* tap into the greatness of each and every one of us.

This chapter focuses on the actions we can take to help these students achieve "wellness" in all six dimensions: intellectual, physical, psychological, emotional, spiritual, and occupational. Educators can revitalize communities and cities, and put "hope" back into so many lives, and so many neighborhoods.

## One Final Attitude Check

Teaching can (and should) bring satisfaction. Teachers are more likely to feel frustrated and dissatisfied, however, when

- they don't feel they are "reaching certain children."

- they are not rewarded (professionally, personally, or financially) for the children they have reached and the achievement gains they have facilitated.

- they lose "control" of their classrooms.

- they are "disrespected" by either colleagues, supervisors, students, or parents.

- they do not receive support from within the school or school systems.

- their efforts don't seem to be making a difference in the quality of life for their students.

With appropriate strategies, teachers can make a significant difference in the quality of life for their Black and Hispanic students. They can reach more students, derive more personal and professional gratification for a job well done, and maintain control of a respectful classroom. The results are less frustration, and more respect from colleagues, supervisors, and parents.

Instructional strategies which *can* make a difference are, however, often not easily implemented. Attitudes and behaviors born of habit-forming procedures and actions are not easily changed. Teachers must be *ready* for attitudinal and behavioral change before any attempts to implement the ideas presented in this book can be successful. Often, teachers find themselves half-heartedly implementing new strategies, but maintaining resistant attitudes such as:

- "This won't work with these children."

- "I tried something similar to this before."

- "This is too much trouble."

- "I just don't think I can do it the way they say it should be done."

- "What if—after all of my efforts—nothing happens?"

- "I'd try some of these suggestions if I had more time."

- "Why do I have to be the one who changes?"

- "You just can't teach an old dog new tricks"

Are any of these *your* excuses?

You have a golden opportunity to uplift countless students who *NEED* what you have to give. *YOU* need an attitude that knows no limitations to your power. Take time now to reassess how you really feel about the following:

### a) The urgency of the problem . . .

If you're thinking that the underachievement of Black and Hispanic students can best be corrected by *others* (not you), or if you feel that the presence of such a "tiny percentage" of Black and Hispanic youth in your school is reason to take the problem lightly, you're in for a rude awakening. The appreciation of cultural diversity and the implementation of pluralistic curricula will benefit all students and should take place *even in all-White classrooms*. Otherwise, we perpetuate cultural and racial alienation and bigotry.

### b) How you develop and communicate your expectations of Black and Hispanic students . . .

Are you able to deal effectively with differences and diversity in students? To what extent do you allow differences in student race, class, looks, speech, placement, behavior, or achievement to influence your opinions and expectations? Some teachers may innocently or inadvertently communicate negative feelings to students who can only judge the teachers by their behavior. Each teacher must determine whether he or she has engaged in verbal or nonverbal behavior which can send a negative message of low expectations to a particular student.

### c) How significantly do you value your role in augmenting the academic self-image of your Black and Hispanic students . . .

Teachers must appreciate not only the role they play in sharing knowledge, they must also see their interactions with all students as meaningful and motivational. As a professional, you must often take the first (and even second) step in saving the lives of students who are not meeting their full academic potential.

### d) How much effort are you willing to put forth in facilitating the eradication of institutional racism in your school or school system . . .

Educators must push for more pluralistic curricula and an elimination of tracking and ability grouping, as well as more appropriate assessment instruments and procedures for Black and Hispanic students.

### e) How willing are you to change your style of teaching . . .

If you understand that learning style differences can significantly debilitate Black and Hispanic student performance, you would be defeating your purpose in being a teacher if you didn't seek to facilitate congruence between their learning styles and your teaching style.

### f) Can you truthfully say you see something in all students to like and to enhance . . .

Unless teachers can lift up our children and give *them* genuine hope for a better future, children may be alienated and lose their motivation to live a meaningful life. Unless they feel a bond with school personnel and develop confidence—through appreciation of their strengths—fear of failure will keep many of them from ever realizing their self worth and full potential. Moreover, many will develop a greater aversion for "mainstream society" and the success principles needed for legitimate survival if they start seeing teachers as "the enemy".

### g) Are you willing to set personal goals and help Black and Hispanic youth do the same . . .

Educators should want professional gratification as well as the joy of building student bonds. It's important to set short- and long-term goals and priorities. Are teachers paid just to impart knowledge, or to develop thriving, successful human beings? Greater teaching satisfaction is derived through the establishment of professional goals and benchmarks for goal fulfillment.

### h) Are you willing to establish the appropriate climate for student growth . . .

This will require more creativity, better communication skills, enthusiasm, and an emphasis on building determination, diligence, and discipline. It also means resorting to behavior that neither demeans, degrades, nor destroys the student's desire to do well.

### i) Are you willing to be more innovative in establishing good student discipline . . .

Prevention strategies designed to enhance student motivation can improve student responsibility, self-control, and discipline. Yet, their implementation requires commitment, persistence, and consistency.

### j) How far are you willing to go to build effective partnerships with home and community . . .

The achievement and discipline of Black and Hispanic students are improved when communities become a part of the education process.[1] Teachers and schools can be the catalysts which foster the shared values and commitments of a community to its youth. No society can remain vital without a reasonable base of shared values. Such values are not established by edict from lofty levels of the society, however. They are generated chiefly in the family, *school*, church or other intimate settings in which people deal with one another face to face."[2] Schools (and their teachers and administrators) must be willing to do whatever it takes to garner requisite community support.

### k) What are you willing to do to improve both equality and equity in education and access to opportunities for Black and Hispanic students . . .

While we know that school desegregation and test bias have contributed to a lack of equity in our schools,[3] this is no reason to run from opportunities to inspire diverse youth to overcome obstacles in their lives in their personal pursuit of excellence.

## Helping Youth to Develop Success Habits

Teachers can help youth to focus on the future, and to overcome setbacks and adversity. In his book, *Think and Grow Rich: A Black Choice*, Dennis Kimbro observes that while racial oppression and discrimination still exist, they should not keep Blacks or Hispanics from losing sight of the "greater battle," and developing themselves as individuals.[4] In teaching Black and Hispanic youth to live inside and "outside" of their culture, teachers can help these students understand that "Greatness is not measured by what a man or woman accomplishes, but by the opposition he or she has overcome to reach his goal."[5]

The academic self-image of some Black and Hispanic youth may be so low they do not have the self-love needed to overcome real and perceived obstacles. A good and loving teacher can open the door to student self-love and motivation. A good teacher can help a student strengthen his personal resolve to use the talents he has to be a success. A good and effective teacher can help students gain knowledge and appreciation of countless others who have also overcome seemingly insurmountable odds in their quest for greatness.

It would certainly be helpful if teachers shared with students the success principles outlined by Kimbro. Those principles include:[6]

- using the imagination wisely and putting ideas into action.

- having a burning desire to succeed and the right "attitude."

- having faith—the prerequisite to power

- developing persistence skills.

- developing a strong sense of self-worth.

- developing self-reliance and a better use of individual fortitude.

- developing a pleasing personality.

- getting and maintaining enthusiasm.

- setting goals and staying on track.

- developing and expanding the potential of the mind.

Teachers can help students appreciate these principles by developing classroom activities and assignments around the application of these principles to everyday life.

Marva Collins once observed you should teach as if your life depended on it.[7] And in a real sense, it does. No one ever said teaching was easy. Your ability to put ideas into practice with a goal of preparing all students for meaningful futures—can make teaching the most rewarding thing you could ever do.

## Conclusions and Impact

I am convinced that anyone who endeavors to develop children is a *true* hero/heroine. Not only do I believe in teachers, I revere them. I know how overwhelming the challenge of developing individuals can appear to be at times. But the *real* challenge is the challenge of commitment. When more teachers increase their commitment, and their repertoire of teaching techniques, more students will be able to succeed and more educators will reap the *real* joy this profession is capable of providing.

Hopefully, educators who read this book will be inspired. They will immediately put into practice most of the ideas I have presented. Hopefully, practitioners will not give up on these students; but more importantly, educators must not give up on themselves. Success *is* the "progressive" realization of a worthwhile goal. As long as you are willing to persist, you need not worry, you *WILL* experience success and the subsequent *JOY* that comes when you know you've changed a life.

Rather than ignore the problem or run from the challenge, rather than lament all of the telltale signs of human, moral, and social decay in our communities, educators can facilitate long-term problem resolution. The problems wrought by the underachievement of so many Black and Hispanic youth will continue to escalate unless there is a total school effort for abatement. If I didn't believe in the gratifying GREATNESS and ability of educators, I would not have written this book. My prayer is that every reader is inspired to dig just a little deeper. You deserve the good feeling that professional excellence and student success is sure to bring.

Not only must you believe you can make a difference—you must *choose* to make a difference.

GOOD LUCK!

# Notes

1. Duff, O.B., and McClain, H.J. eds. *Student Concerns: Discipline, Academic Achievement and Community Involvement in a Desegregated Setting.* Proceedings (December 13-14, 1979), Bethesda, MD ERIC Document Reproduction Services, ED 210362, 1981.

2. Gardner, J.W. *Building Communities.* Paper presented to the Independent Sector of Washington, D.C., 1991. Reprinted in Raspberry, W. "Reclaiming Community" *The Washington Post*, February 9, 1992.

3. Green, R.L. and Griffore, R.J. "School Desegregation, Testing and the Urgent Need for Equity" in *Education* 99 (Fall 1978): 16-19.

4. Kimbro, D. & Hill, N. *Think and Grow Rich: A Black Choice*, New York: Ballentine Books, 1991.

5. Ibid.

6. Ibid.

7. Collins, M., *Marva Collins' Way.* Los Angeles: Jeremy P. Tarcher, Inc., 1990.

# 9 FOCUSING ON YOUR EFFORTS

*He who knows the why of living surmounts every how...*

Nietzche

I hope this book has satisfied your understanding of *why* you are so important in facilitating the success of Black and Hispanic students. How you go about fulfilling your professional responsibilities—from this day forward—will say much about you, both as a person and as a professional.

The following worksheets can be used to assist you in your endeavors to bring out the best in Black and Hispanic children by giving the *very best* of yourself.

**Worksheet A, "Indicators of Poor Student Self-Image,"** can help a teacher determine whether a student has a low academic self-image, a low social self-image, or both.

**Worksheet B, "Teacher Behaviors That Improve Achievement Motivation in Students,"** can serve as a self-evaluation, and provide the opportunity for teachers to improve their total approach to increasing student achievement and development.

**Worksheet C, "Student Activities that Enhance Self-Concept,"** includes activities to help students improve their self-image and their academic achievement.

| WORSHEET A | | | |
|---|---|---|---|

### WORKSHEET A
### Indicators of Poor Student Self-Image

Here are a number of characteristics of a poor self-concept in children and youth, which are grouped into academic and social behaviors. Use this list to assess how you can best help an individual child strengthen academic and social self-concepts.

| Check the appropriate column on the right.<br>**F** = Frequently          **S** = Sometimes          **R** = Rarely | F | S | R |
|---|---|---|---|
| **POOR ACADEMIC SELF-IMAGE**<br>*To what extent does the student . . .* | | | |
| 1.   fail to complete work? | | | |
| 2.   show hostile behavior? | | | |
| 3.   use defiant speech? | | | |
| 4.   daydream? | | | |
| 5.   show little or no eye contact? | | | |
| 6.   make excuses? | | | |
| 7.   give up too easily? | | | |
| 8.   skip school or is tardy? | | | |
| 9.   fail to volunteer or participate? | | | |
| 10.   is withdrawn and isolated? | | | |
| 11.   express dislike for school, the teacher, or both? | | | |
| 12.   exhibit facial expressions and body movements that show frustration, anxiety, or pain? | | | |

| | F | S | R |
|---|---|---|---|
| **WORKSHEET A**<br>**Indicators of Poor Student Self-Image (Continued)** | | | |
| **POOR SOCIAL SELF-IMAGE**<br>*To what extent does the student . . .* | | | |
| 1. lack confidence in performing before others? | | | |
| 2. fail to demonstrate ability in such social skills as sports, dancing, "playing the dozens," or rapping? | | | |
| 3. function in a support group of peers? | | | |
| 4. exhibit interest in social activities such as dancing, listening to music, or sports activities? | | | |
| 5. show little or no eye contact? | | | |
| 6. persist in learning social skills (bike riding, card playing, music, or sports)? | | | |
| 7. demonstrate friendly, sincere behavior? | | | |
| 8. dress slovenly and show poor personal hygiene? | | | |
| 9. have poor nutritional habits? | | | |
| 10. try too hard to please? | | | |
| 11. cry easily? | | | |
| 12. use facial expressions and body language that show pain, anxiety, or frustration? | | | |

## WORKSHEET B
### Teacher Behaviors that Improve Achievement Motivation in Students

Here is a self-checklist that you can use to determine your strengths in improving achievement motivation in youth, and areas in which you may want to expand your knowledge and skills. There are two categories:

❑ Check "+" if you are comfortable with your knowledge and skills in this area and exhibit appropriate and consistent behavior.

❑ Check "–" if you need to strengthen your knowledge and skills and to demonstrate appropriate behaviors consistently.

| CREATING A MULTICULTURAL ENVIRONMENT<br>*As a teacher, how do you rate yourself on:* | + | – |
|---|---|---|
| 1. reviewing reading materials and school tests to identify culturally sensitive materials and taking steps to minimize their impact on students? | | |
| 2. identifying and bringing to the attention of school officials any policies or procedures that inadvertently penalize certain races, cultures, sexes, or disabilities? | | |
| 3. understanding and teaching African-American and Hispanic-American history and culture? | | |
| 4. developing classroom activities that foster an understanding and appreciation of the struggle of Black Americans against slavery? | | |
| 5. providing opportunities for students of different racial and ethnic groups to interact? | | |
| 6. identifying and discussing in class contemporary examples of overt racism (e.g., South Africa)? | | |
| 7. integrating appreciation for cultural diversity into all of your classroom activities? | | |
| 8. recognizing and pointing out to students values that strengthen cultural bonds? | | |
| 9. constructing and using heterogeneous groups? | | |
| 10. distinguishing between equality and equity and knowing when to treat students the same or differently on the basis of their race, ethnic group, disability, culture, sex, or level of academic achievement? | | |

| WORKSHEET B<br>Teacher Behaviors that Improve Achievement Motivation in Students (Continued) | | |
|---|---|---|
| | + | – |
| 11. allowing students to engage in activities that will enhance their appreciation of the cultural strengths of all diverse groups? | | |
| **USING A VARIETY OF TEACHING STYLES**<br>*As a teacher, how do you rate yourself on:* | | |
| 1. encouraging personal interaction, including hugs, touching, and affectionate pats? | | |
| 2. identifying students' strengths and weaknesses in *how* they learn? | | |
| 3. using instructional strategies that allow students to build on their strengths and overcome their weaknesses? | | |
| 4. explaining how class content is related to the students' experiences? | | |
| 5. encouraging more student grouping and interaction that lead to greater student achievement and appreciation of diversity? | | |
| 6. developing rapport with each of your students? | | |
| 7. conducting classroom activities that allow for the emotional and physical involvement of Black and Hispanic youth? | | |
| 8. using positive slogans and inspirational messages all over the classroom? | | |
| 9. making use of the buddy system? | | |
| 10. using eye contact in a supportive way? | | |
| 11. organizing curriculum around central ideas and themes? | | |
| 12. organizing math instruction around major mathematical processes of abstracting, inventing, proving, and applying? | | |
| 13. using alternative instructional strategies, e.g., cooperative learning and peer coaching? | | |
| **USING COOPERATIVE AND FLEXIBLE GROUPING**<br>*As a teacher, how do you rate yourself on:* | | |
| 1. using heterogeneous grouping rather than ability grouping and tracking? | | |

## WORKSHEET B
### Teacher Behaviors that Improve Achievement Motivation in Students (Continued)

| | + | − |
|---|---|---|
| 2. using more diagnostic pre-testing to enhance the heterogeneous grouping process? | | |
| 3. providing more opportunities for teacher-student interaction? | | |
| 4. employing some forms of cooperative learning groups? | | |
| 5. setting up and using a peer tutoring or coaching system? | | |
| 6. using a greater variety of learning materials and activities? | | |
| 7. providing more frequent use of high quality feedback? | | |
| 8. re-grouping students at regular intervals? | | |

### TEACHING HIGHER ORDER THINKING SKILLS
*As a teacher, how do you rate yourself on:*

| | | |
|---|---|---|
| 1. using open-ended and essay questions that foster active involvement and reflections? | | |
| 2. providing opportunities for critical thinking through open-ended questions? | | |
| 3. providing opportunities for divergent thinking by asking students to compare and contrast? | | |
| 4. providing opportunities for inductive thinking by specifically asking students to reason from the specific to the general? | | |
| 5. providing opportunities for deductive thinking by specifically asking students to reason from the general to the specific? | | |
| 6. using one-to-one cajoling, probing, delving, and inspiring to get children to develop their thinking powers? | | |
| 7. allowing students to differentiate, integrate, and reintegrate so as to develop representational competence? | | |
| 8. providing opportunities for higher level distancing and metacognitive activities? | | |
| 9. providing opportunities for more role plays, simulation planning, and evaluations? | | |
| 10. providing regular opportunities for problem solving? | | |

| | + | − |
|---|---|---|
| **WORSHEET B** | | |

**WORKSHEET B**
**Teacher Behaviors that Improve Achievement Motivation in Students (Continued)**

| | + | − |
|---|---|---|
| **OVERCOMING FEAR OF FAILURE AND REJECTION OF SUCCESS**<br>*As a teacher, how do you rate yourself on:* | | |
| 1. identifying students' unique talents and non-academic strengths and building on those to foster confidence and overcome academic weaknesses? | | |
| 2. using peers positively to identify strengths and encourage success through group activities? | | |
| 3. using the buddy system? | | |
| 4. developing a positive and cooperative relationship with the parent or guardian? | | |
| 5. celebrating individual student accomplishments throughout the school year? | | |
| 6. helping students set short- and long-range goals? | | |
| 7. allowing for weekly reviews of famous Black and Hispanic Americans who have set goals and achieved them? | | |
| 8. setting monthly academic achievement goals for each child which can be shared with parents or guardians? | | |
| 9. using "The Success Chart"? | | |
| 10. using activities to improve success motivation? | | |
| **IMPROVING THE TOTAL COMMITMENT**<br>*As a teacher, how do you rate yourself on:* | | |
| 1. projecting an image that tells students that you are here to build rather than destroy them as persons? | | |
| 2. letting students know that you are aware of and interested in them as individuals? | | |
| 3. conveying your experiences and confidence that each student can meet well-defined standards of values and demands for competence and can follow guidance toward solutions or problems? | | |
| 4. enhancing the academic expectations and evaluations that parents or guardians hold of their children's ability? | | |

**WORKSHEET B**
**Teacher Behaviors that Improve Achievement Motivation in Students (Continued)**

| | + | − |
|---|---|---|
| 5.  serving as a model of sensitivity and high ideals for each student? | | |
| 6.  taking every opportunity to establish effective private (one-on-one) or semi-private communications with students? | | |
| 7.  encouraging students to express their opinions and ideas? | | |
| 8.  conveying to students concern and interest for their needs? | | |
| 9.  making certain the classroom climate is inviting physically and emotionally? | | |
| 10.  exhibiting enthusiasm for learning tasks and for the students? | | |
| 11.  interjecting humor into the classroom? | | |
| 12.  making a concerted effort to interact with each student? | | |
| 13.  encouraging students to praise their peers? | | |
| 14.  setting realistic but challenging expectations for students? | | |
| 15.  showing a desire to learn more about the various cultures represented in your classroom? | | |
| 16.  providing opportunities for all students to "shine"? | | |
| 17.  working with each student to establish goals, develop strengths, and overcome weaknesses? | | |

**PROMOTING IMPROVED STUDENT DISCIPLINE**
*As a teacher, how do you rate yourself on:*

| | | |
|---|---|---|
| 1.  having a positive attitude and a genuine "like" for all students? | | |
| 2.  building on the non-academic strengths of all students? | | |
| 3.  providing students with tasks to improve their sense of responsibility? | | |
| 4.  showing respect, trust, a caring attitude, and a loving touch? | | |
| 5.  punishing student behavior rather than students? | | |
| 6.  using disciplinary actions to instruct rather than to punish? | | |
| 7.  rewarding and complimenting students for good behavior? | | |

| | | + | − |
|---|---|---|---|
| **WORKSHEET B** <br> **Teacher Behaviors that Improve Achievement Motivation in Students (Continued)** | | | |
| 8. | developing creative and effective alternatives to suspension? | | |
| **IMPROVING THE SCHOOL AND CLASSROOM CLIMATE** <br> *As a teacher, how do you rate yourself on:* | | | |
| 1. | using bright, warm, and decorative classroom colors? | | |
| 2. | highlighting accomplishments of local heroes/heroines? | | |
| 3. | displaying individual work and accomplishments of all students? | | |
| 4. | fostering mutual trust and respect between students? | | |
| 5. | fostering mutual helpfulness between students? | | |
| 6. | moving around the class so that all students feel greater physical proximity with you? | | |
| 7. | monitoring student progress? | | |
| 8. | fostering freedom of student expression? | | |
| 9. | showing empathic understanding? | | |
| 10. | showing an interest in the child as a person? | | |
| **HOW DO YOU RATE YOUR SCHOOL ON:** | | | |
| 1. | developing in all school personnel a positive commitment to student achievement? | | |
| 2. | setting appropriate standards for student behavior? | | |
| 3. | maintaining a purposeful, safe, and orderly environment? | | |
| **STRENGTHENING THE HOME–SCHOOL BOND** <br> *As a teacher, how do you rate yourself on:* | | | |
| 1. | understanding that parental involvement should encompass more than "at home" responsibilities? | | |
| 2. | relating to parents with an attitude that conveys respect? | | |
| 3. | making positive telephone calls with "good" news on student behavior? | | |
| 4. | helping parents to understand that your role is to help the child grow in many ways? | | |

| WORKSHEET B<br>Teacher Behaviors that Improve Achievement Motivation in Students (Continued) | + | − |
|---|---|---|
| 5.  educating more parents about the school's expectations of them? | | |
| 6.  sharing information with parents that will build understanding, knowledge, and trust? | | |
| 7.  encouraging parents to become a part of established parent organizations? | | |
| 8.  pushing for annual "Family Nights" in your school? | | |
| 9.  finding and using other resources in the community? | | |
| 10.  making use of community role models and mentors? | | |
| 11.  creating partnerships with community businesses and other youth-serving organizations, agencies, or institutions? | | |

Adapted from Kuykendal, C. *Improving Black Student Achievement by Enhancing Student Self-Image,* Mid-Atlantic Equity Center of American University, Washington, D.C. 1989.

## WORKSHEET C
### Student Activities that Enhance Self-Concept

Here are some activities for students that enhance self-concept. If you regularly provide this activity in your classroom, check the blank on the left. If you don't provide opportunities for this activity, check the blank on the right. You may want to expand your repertoire if you have more checks on the right than you have on the left.

**Provide**                                                        **Don't Provide**

❏   1.   Activities where students can entertain classmates and/or display   ❏
non-academic talents and strengths as well as academic gifts.

❏   2.   Activities where students can engage in such social skills as   ❏
dancing, sports events, rapping, singing, or dramatic readings.

❏   3.   Peer tutoring and group projects where students can develop   ❏
mutually supportive systems with peers.

❏   4.   Practical skills which allow students to repeat in rhyme.   ❏

❏   5.   Non-structured, challenging games; puzzles; activities with no   ❏
deadline for completion.

❏   6.   Activities designed to help students be successful by working on   ❏
challenging yet achievable goals.

❏   7.   Activities involving the use of pantomime.   ❏

❏   8.   Multicultural subject content and activities.   ❏

❏   9.   Activities to foster concentration and long attention spans.   ❏

❏   10.   Learning centers relating to subject matter and student interests.   ❏

❏   11.   Activities that explore different types of families and the cultural   ❏
strengths of each.

❏   12.   Activities which highlight the unique strengths and special talents   ❏
of each student.

# BIBLIOGRAPHY

Akbar, N'aim. Address Before the Black Child Development Institute. Annual Meeting, San Francisco, CA, October 1975.

American Association of Colleges for Teacher Education. "No One Model American." Washington, D.C., 1973.

American Council on Education/Education Commission on Minority Participation in Education and American Life. *One Third of a Nation.* Washington, D.C., May 1988.

Banks, J. and Grombs, J. eds. *Black Self-Concept.* New York: McGraw-Hill Book Co., 1972.

Beane, D. *Mathematics and Science: Critical Fillers for the Future of Minority Students.* Washington, D.C.: Mid-Atlantic Equity Center, American University, 1988.

Bell, Jr., C. "Exploring the Progressively Decreasing Scores on Comprehensive Tests of Basic Skills (CTBS) of the School Children of the District of Columbia Public Schools as They Progress from Elementary School into High School." Alexandria, VA ERIC Document Reproduction Service ED 226234, 1985.

Benham-Tye, B. "Heterogeneous Grouping in High School." *Educational Leadership*, December 1984.

Berube, M. *Education and Poverty: Effective Schooling in the U.S.* Westport, CT: Greenwood Press, 1984.

Brendtro, L., Brokenleg, M. and Van Bockern, S. *Reclaiming Youth At Risk*. Bloomington, IN: National Education Service, 1990.

Carnegie Council on Adolescent Development. "Turning Points: Education in American in the 21st Century." Washington, D.C. 1989.

Cheyney, L., Fine, M., Ravitch, D. *American Memory: A Report on the Humanities in the Nations Public Schools*. National Endowment for the Humanities, 1987.

Children's Defense Fund. *Black and White Children in America: Key Facts*. Washington, D.C.

Choy, S.J. and Dodd, D.H. "Standard-English Speaking and Non-Standard Hawaiian on English-speaking Children: Comprehension of Both Dialects and Teachers' Evaluations." *Journal of Educational Psychology* 68, April 1976, pp. 184-193.

Clifford, M.N., and Walster, E. "Research Note: The Effect of Physical Attractiveness in Teacher Expectations. *Sociology of Education* 46 Spring 1973, pp. 248-58.

Collins, M. *Marva Collins' Way*. Los Angeles, CA: Jeremy P. Tarcher, Inc. 1990.

Cooper, H.M., et al. "Understanding Pygmalion: The Social Psychology of Self-Fulfilling Classroom Expectations." Alexandria, VA ERIC Document Reproduction Service, ED 182642, 1979.

Cooper, H.M., Baron, R.M. and Louie, C.A. "The Importance of Race and Social Class Information in the Formation of Expectancies About Academic Performance." *Journal of Educational Psychology* 67, 1975.

Council on Interracial Books for Children. *Fact Sheets on Institutional Racism*. New York: Council on Interracial Books for Children, 1984.

Denbo, S. *Improving Minority Student Achievement: Focus on the Classroom*. Washington, D.C.: Mid-Atlantic Equity Center, American University, 1986.

Dickerman, M. "Teaching Cultural Pluralism" in Banks, J. *Teaching Ethnic Studies*. Taken from Gay, G."Achieving Educational Equality Through Curriculum Desegregation." *Phi Delta Kappan* Sept. 1990.

Duff, O.B. and McClain, H.J., eds. *Student Concerns: Discipline, Academic Achievement and Community Involvement in a Desegregated Setting*. Proceedings (December 13-14, 1979). Bethesda, MD ERIC Document Reproduction Service, ED 210362, 1981.

Dunken, M.J. and Biddle, B.J. *The Study of Teaching*. New York: Holt, Rinehart and Winston, 1974.

Edmonds, R. "Effective Schools and the Urban Poor." *Educational Leadership* October 1979.

Edmonds, R. "Some Schools Work and More Can" in *Social Policy* 1979, Vol. 9.

Fagen, J. and Jones, S.J. "Toward a Theoretical Model for Intervention with Violent Juvenile Offenders" in Mathias, R. *Violent Juvenile Offenders*. San Francisco, CA: National Council on Crime and Delinquency, 1984.

Fair, G.W. "Coping with Double-Barrelled Discrimination." *Journal of School Health* 50 May 1980.

Fine, M. Why Urban Adolescents Drop Into and Out of Public Schools. *Teacher College Board*, Spring 1986.

Forham, S. and Ozbu, J. "Black Students' School Success: Coping with the Burden of Acting White." *The Urban Review* Vol. 18, No. 3, 1986.

Gardner, J.W. *Building Communities*. Paper presented to the Independent Sector of Washington, D.C. 1991. Reprinted in Raspberry, W. "Reclaiming Community." *The Washington Post*, February 9, 1992, p. A20.

Garret-Holiday, B. "Differential Effects of Children's Self-Perceptions and Teachers' Perceptions on Black Children's Academic Achievement." *Journal of Negro Education*, Vol. 54, No. 1, 1985.

Gay, G. "Achieving Educational Equality Through Curriculum Desegregation." *Phi Delta Kappan*, Sept. 1990.

Gilbert, S. and Gay, G. "Improving the Success in School of Poor Black Children." *Phi Delta Kappan*, October 1985.

Gilmore, J. and E. *Give Your Child a Future.* Englewood Cliffs, N.J.: Prentice Hall, Inc., 1982.

Ginott, Haim. *Between Teacher and Child.* New York: The Macmillan Company, 1972.

Glasgow, D. *The Black Underclass: Poverty, Unemployment and Entrapment of Ghetto Youth.* San Francisco: Josset Base Limited, 1980.

Good, T.L. "Teacher Expectations and Student Perceptions: A Decade of Research." *Educational Leadership,* Vol. 38, February 1981, pp. 415-22.

Good, T.L. and Brophy, J.E. *Looking in Classrooms.* New York, NY: Harper and Row Publishers, 1973.

Graves, E. "Public Education: Broken Promise for Many." *Black Enterprise,* September 1978.

Green, R.L. and Griffore, R.J. "School Desegregation, Testing and the Urgent Need for Equity" in *Education* 99, Fall, 1978: 16-19.

Gullub, W.L. and Sloan, E. "Teacher Expectations and Race and Socioeconomic Status." *Urban Education* 13, April 1978, pp. 95-106.

Hale-Benson, J. *Black Children: Their Roots, Culture and Learning Styles.* Provo, UT: Brigham Young University Press, 1982.

Hammond, L. *Equality and Excellence: Educational Status of Black Americans*. New York: The College Board, 1985.

Hare, B. *Black Girls: A Comparative Analysis of Self Perceptions and Achievement by Race, Sex and Socioeconomic Background*. Baltimore: Johns Hopkins University, 1979.

Harrischefeger, A. and Wiley, P.E. "A Merit Assessment of Vocational Education Programs in Secondary Schools." A Statement to the Subcommittee on Elementary, Secondary and Vocational Education, September 1980.

Henderson, A. *The Evidence Continues to Grow: Parent Involvement Improves Student Achievement*. Columbia, MD: National Committee for Citizens in Education, 1987.

Henderson, A., Marburger, C., Oams, T. *Beyond the Bake Sale: An Educators Guide to Working With Parents*. Columbia, MD: National Committee for Citizens in Education, 1989.

Hilliard, A.G. III. *Alternatives to I.Q. Testing: An Approach to the Identification of Gifted Minority Children: Final Report to the California State Department of Education*, 1976.

Hilliard, A.G. III. "Cultural Diversity and Special Education." *Exceptional Children* 46 (May 1980): 584-88.

Howard, B. *Learning to Persist, Persisting to Learn*. Washington, D.C.: Mid-Atlantic Equity Center of American University, 1987.

Howard, J. "Race and How it Affects Our Every Day Life." *Detroit Free Press*, December 12, 1985.

Irvin, J.J. "Teacher Communication Patterns As Related to the Race and Sex of the Student." *Journal of Educational Research*, July/August 1985.

Johnson, P., Johnson R., Holubec, E. and Ray, P. *Circles of Learning—Cooperation in the Classroom*. Alexandria, VA: Association for Supervision and Curriculum Development. 1986.

Johnson, P., Johnson R., Holubec, E. and Ray, P. *Circles of Learning—Cooperation in the Classroom*. Alexandria, VA: Association for Supervision and Curriculum Development. 1986.

Jones, K. "The Black Male in Jeopardy" in *The Crisis*, 1986, V. 93, n. 3.

Kagan, S. Cooperative Learning Resources for Teachers. Laguan Niguel, CA: Resources for Teachers, 1989.

Kimbro, D. and Hill, N. *Think and Grow Rich: A Black Choice*. New York: Fawcett Columbine, 1991.

Knowles, L. and Prewitt, K. *Institutional Racism in America*. Englewood Cliffs, N.J.: Prince-Hall, 1969.

Kozol, J. *Illiterate America*. New York: Plume Books, 1985.

Kunjufu, J. *Countering the Conspiracy to Destroy Black Boys*. African-American Images, Chicago, IL 1985.

Kunjufu, J. *The Conspiracy to Destroy Black Boys*. Chicago: African-American Images, 1985.

Kuykendall, C. *Developing Leadership for Parent/Citizen Groups*. Columbia, MD: National Committee for Citizens in Education, 1976.

Kuykendall, C. *Improving Black Student Achievement By Enhancing Student Self-Image*. Washington, D.C.: American University, Mid-Atlantic Equity Center, 1989.

Kuykendall, C. Unpublished Study of the Responses of Over 2000 Teachers on Needs and Attitudes, 1984-1987 in the Washington, D.C. Metropolitan Area.

Kuykendall, C. *You and Yours: Making the Most of This School Year*. Washington, D.C.: Mid-Atlantic Equity Center of American University, 1987.

Lawler, J.M. I.Q., *Heredity and Racism*. New York: International Publishers, 1978.

Lazar, I. and Darlington, R. *Summary: Lasting Effects After Pre-School*. Ithaca, NY: Cornell University, 1978.

Levin, H.M. and Schutze, E., eds. Financing Recurrent Education: Strategies for Improving Employment, Job Opportunities and Productivity. Beverly Hills, CA: Sage Publications 1983.

Lezotte, L.W. and Bancroft, B.A. "School Improvement Based on Effective Schools' Research: A Promising Approach for Economically Disadvantaged Minority Students." *Journal of Negro Education* 54, Summer 1985, pp. 301-12.

Lippit, R. and others. "An Inter-Center Program for Studies in Children, Youth and Family Life." Survey Research Center and the Research Center for Group Dynamics. Ann Arbor, MI, University of Michigan, n.d.

Little, R. "Basic Education of Socialization in the Armed Forces." *American Journal of Orthopsychiatry*, October 1968.

Madhubuti, H. *Black Men: Obsolete, Single, Dangerous?* Chicago: Third World Press, 1990.

Marks, W. *Strategies for Educational Change: Recognizing the Gifts and Talents of All Children*. New York: Macmillan Publishing Co., 1981.

Martin, R. *Teaching Through Encouragement*. Englewood Cliffs, N.J.: Prince Hall, Inc., 1980.

Massachusetts Advocacy Center. "States Report—Freedom of Information in Massachusetts." Boston, MA. March 1975.

Mathias, Robert, editor. *Violent Youth Offenders*. San Francisco: National Council on Crime and Delinquency. 1984.

McClelland, D. "Sources of an Achievement" in McClelland, P. and Steele, R. (editors). *Human Motivation*. Morristown, N.J.: General Learning Press, 1973.

Mitchell, W. and Conn, C.P. *Power of Positive Students*. New York: Morrow Publishing Co., 1985.

Morgan, E. *Inequality in Classroom Learning: Schooling and Democratic Citizenship.* New York: Praeger, 1977.

Morgan, H. "How Schools Fail Black Children." *Social Policy,* Jan-Feb, 1980.

Munroe, M.J. "Effective Teacher Behavior as an Avenue to Enhance the Self-Esteem of Teachers. Bethesda, MD, ERIC Document Reproduction Service, ED 228162, 1982.

Murnane, R. "Empirical Analysis of the Relations Between School Resources and the Cognitive Development of Black Inner City Youth Children in A Large Urban School System (New Haven)". Taken from"Final Report on Schooling of Young Children Cognitive and Affective Outcomes." National Institute of Education, 1975.

Murray, H.B., Herling, B.B. and Staebler, B.K. "The Effects of Locus of Control and Pattern of Performance on Teacher Evaluation of a Student." *Psychology in the Schools* 10, 1973: 345-50.

National Center for Improved Science Education: Getting Americans Started in Science: A Blueprint for Science Education in Elementary School. *Prepublication copy,* July 1989.

National Council of La Raza. *State of Hispanic America*, 1991.

National Urban League. *State of Black America*, New York: 1983, 1986, 1989, 1991.

Oakes, J. "Keeping Track: The Policy and Practice of Curriculum Inequality." *Phi Delta Kappan.*

Olsen, G. and Moore, M. *Voices from the Classroom*, Oakland, CA, Citizens Policy Center, 1986.

Parker, W. "I Ain't No Group, I'm Me." *Strategies in Educational Change.* Macmillan Press, 1981.

Perkins, U.E. *Home is a Dirty Street: The Social Oppression of Black Children.* Chicago: Third World Press, 1975.

Poussaint, A. and Atkinson, C. "Black Youth and Motivation" in *Black Self-Concept*. Edited by Banks, J. and Grambs, J.D., New York: McGraw Hill Book Co., 1972.

Raspberry, W. "Reclaiming Community". *The Washington Post*. February 9, 1992.

Rist, R. "Social Distance and Social Inequality in A Ghetto Kindergarten Classroom." *Urban Education* 7, October 1979.

Robovits, P.C. and Maehr, M.L. "Pygmalion in Black and White." *Journal of Personality and Social Psychology*, 25 February 1973.

Rosenthal, R. and Jacobson, L. *Pygmalion in the Classroom: Teacher Expectations and Pupil's Intellectual Development*. New York: Holt, Rinehart and Winston, 1968.

Sadker, D. and Sadker, M. "Is the OK Classroom OK?" *Phi Delta Kappan* 66, January 1985.

Sadler, M. and D. & Long, L. "Gender and Educational Equality" in Banks, J. and C.A., eds. *Multicultural Education Issues and Perspectives*. Boston: Allyn and Bacon, 1989.

Shoop, R. "Increasing Citizen Participation thru Community Education." Education Digest. April 1985.

Silberman, C. *Crisis in the Classroom*. New York: Vintage Books, 1971.

Slavin, R. *Student Team Learning*. Washington, D.C.: NEA Professional Library 1986.

Smith, R.P. and Denton, J.J. "The Effects of Dialect Ethnicity and Orientation to Sociolinguistics on the Perception of Teaching Candidates." *Educational Research Quarterly* 3 Spring 1980, pp. 70-79.

Taylor, O. *Cross-Cultural Miscommunication*. Mid-Atlantic Equity Center of American University, Washington, D.C. 1987.

*Time*, "A Generation Lost." December, 1986.

U.S. Bureau of Census, 1986.

U.S. Commission on Civil Rights. *Teachers and Students: Differences in Teacher Interaction with Mexican-American and Anglo Students.* Report V: Mexican-American American Education Study, Washington, D.C. U.S. Government Printing Office, 1973.

U.S. Department of Education. *What Works.* Research about Teaching and Learning, 1989.

U.S. Department of Justice. *Study of Men Age 20-29.* May 1990.

Walberg, H. "Families As Partners in Educational Productivity" in *Phi Delta Kappan.* Vol. 65 no. 6, February 1984. pp. 397-400.

Washington, V. "Racial Differences in Teacher Perceptions of First and Fourth Grade Pupils on Selected Characteristics." *Journal of Negro Education.* Vol. 51, No. 1, Winter 1982, pp. 60-60.

Weinberg, G. and Calero, H. *How to Read A Person Like A Book.* New York: Hawthorn Books, 1971.

Williams, F., Whitehead, J.L. and Miller, L. "Relations Between Language, Attitudes and Teacher Expectancy." *American Educational Research Journal.* 9 Spring 1972.

Williams, J.H. and Muehle, S. Relations Among Student Perception Behavior. *Journal of Negro Education*, Fall 1978, pp. 328-36.

# DO YOU HAVE AN IDEA TO SHARE?

The National Educational Service is always looking for high-quality manuscripts that have practical application for educators and others who work with youth.

Do you have a new, innovative, or especially effective approach to some timely issue? Does one of your colleagues have something burning to say on curriculum development, professionalism in education, excellence in teaching, or some other aspect of education? If so, let us know. We would like to hear from you. Tell us that reading *From Rage to Hope: Strategies for Reclaiming Black & Hispanic Students* gave you an incentive to contact us.

Nancy Shin, Director of Publications
National Educational Service
1610 West Third Street
P.O. Box 8
Bloomington, IN  47402
1-800-733-6786
or
1-812-336-7700

*From Rage to Hope: Strategies for Reclaiming Black & Hispanic Students* is one of the many publications produced by the National Educational Service. Our mission is to provide you and other leaders in education, business, and government with timely, top-quality publications, videos, and conferences. If you have any questions or comments about *From Rage to Hope: Strategies for Reclaiming Black & Hispanic Students* or if you want information on in-service training or professional development on any of the following topics:

Discipline with Dignity
Reclaiming Youth at Risk
Cooperative Learning
Thinking Across the Curriculum
Cooperative Management
Parental Involvement

Contact us at:

National Educational Service
1610 West Third Street
P.O. Box 8
Bloomington, IN 47402
1-800-733-6786
1-800-812-336-7700

# NEED MORE COPIES?

Need more copies of this book? Want your own copy? If so, you can order additional copies of *From Rage to Hope: Strategies for Reclaiming Black & Hispanic Students* by using this form or by calling us at (800) 733-6786 (US only) or (812) 336-7700. Or you can order by FAX at (812) 336-7790.

We guarantee complete satisfaction with all of our materials. If you are not completely satisfied with any NES publication, you may return it to us within 30 days for a full refund.

|  | Quantity | Total |
|---|---|---|
| *From Rage to Hope: Strategies for Reclaiming Black & Hispanic Students* ($19.95 each) | _____ | _____ |
| Shipping: Add $2.00 per copy |  | _____ |
| (There is no shipping charge when you *include* payment with your order) |  |  |
| Indiana residents add 5% sales tax |  | _____ |
| TOTAL |  | _____ |

❏ Check enclosed with order      ❏ Please bill me

❏ VISA, MasterCard, or Discover      ❏ Money order

❏ P.O.#_____

Account No._____ Exp. Date _____

Cardholder _____

Ship to:

Name_____Title _____

Organization _____

Address _____

City_____State_____ ZIP _____

Phone _____

Fax _____

MAIL TO:
National Educational Service
1610 W. Third Street
P.O. Box 8
Bloomington, IN 47402